中国足球的小红书

THE LITTLE RED BOOK OF CHINES

By Dave Twydell

CW00419576

Published by:
Yore Publications
12 The Furrows, Harefield,
Middx. UB9 6AT.

© Dave Twydell 1994

....

British Library Cataloguing-in-Publication Data.
A catalogue record for this book
is available from the British Library.

ISBN 1 874427 80 1

(All modern photographs of the Football Grounds were taken by the Author, those relating to Hong Kong are reproduced by kind permission of the Hong Kong F.A. Ltd.)

Yore Publications specialise in the publication of football books, which are normally of an historic theme. Past titles include the detailed Club histories of Kilmarnock, Southend United, Doncaster Rovers, Colchester United, etc. .... Players *'Who's Who'* books - Newport County, Coventry City, Lincoln City, etc. .... General interest - *'Rejected F.C.'* (several volumes detailing the history of the ex-League clubs in England and Scotland), *'Through The Turnstiles'* (A written and statistical history relating to Football League attendances from 1888 to 1992), *'The Code War'* (A history of the three different football 'codes' in Britain), *'Tommy Taylor of Manchester United'* (A Biography), etc. .... plus Videos on specialist Football subjects.

Newsletters (which detail all current and new titles) are posted free, three times per year. Please send a S.A.E. for your initial copy of the latest Newsletter.

Printed by 'The Book Factory'

Contents

Preface

'Groundhopping' in the football sense, can take a number of different forms. Perhaps the true Groundhopper is a fan who not only visits the ground, but also - in his self-appointed 'rules' - must view a complete match. But the beauty of the groundhopping sport is up to the individual who can make up his own 'rules' to suit himself. My own interpretation has no rules. View the ground is a must, and ideally watch a game there, but circumstances do not always allow for the ideal - and a relatively brief visit to China and Hong Kong makes such an extended 'hop', I can assure you, virtually impossible! With unlimited funds, several months to spare, and a good working knowledge of the language (either, or both, Mandarin and Cantonese), then it is perhaps possible. With less than three weeks, on an organised tour, and a Chinese vocabulary that doesn't extend beyond the phonetic 'knee-how' ('hallo'), then I challenge any groundhopper to glean more than I found possible during my journey during April 1994.

This, however, was a holiday (or put more accurately, an 'experience', as our English guide explained during our briefing after one day in Hong Kong), and therefore the opportunities to observe and question were very limited. From my brief investigations made before departure to the mysterious East, there appeared to be very little information available regarding football concerning China and Hong Kong, and therefore my personal experiences will hopefully improve the knowledge available in these footballing undeveloped nations. It is relatively easy to write a football history of a Club or even a Country, without visiting the subject in question, providing one has access to other suitable literature and/or relevant newspapers. But it is my conviction that such a history is greatly enhanced by a personal visit, however brief, in order to relate the story, based not only on fact, but from personal experience, in order to get a real 'feel' for the subject.

This book is also a travelogue, and has been included not as 'padding', but in order to relate some amusing (and at times somewhat alarming) situations, and especially to emphasise the frustrations and unbelievable difficulties in obtaining knowledge on the spot, and having to be undertaken in a totally alien environment. Should any reader attempt to follow my footsteps, or undertake their own investigations, make no mistake about it, you will need a great deal of determination and stamina (in the latter case both mental and physical), as the appropriate pages will hopefully illustrate.

In respect of the Hong Kong presentation, all stated facts should be correct, largely due to the invaluable help provided by Vincent Yuen - the Chief Executive Officer of the Hong Kong F.A., and the excellent publication by that Country's Association which was issued to commemorate their 75th anniversary. My thanks to Deng Jun Feng of Shanghai and Zhou Wei ('Mike') of the China International Travel Service, Beijing, who were both most helpful, and provided me with much of my 'on the spot' information. Hopefully all statements relating to the Chinese section are also correct, remembering the near complete absence of confirmation from other sources in respect of the very recent and current situation. The reader should be made aware that errors may be included. This warning is given since it is unlikely that anyone will be able to dispute some of the modern facts and figures given! Any of my own suppositions have been suitably noted in the narrative. Most of the pre-war facts (and some of the later ones in respect of the Chinese section) have been taken from the small print-run (and now out of print) book, 'Soccer in China' (by Ken Knight), to whom I am indebted.

So, without further ado, let's start on the journey. After a 12 hour flight we have arrived in Hong Kong, and the adventure is about to begin.......

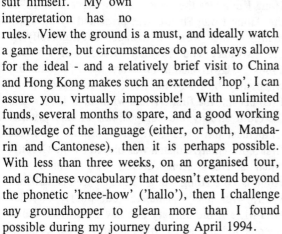

Hong Kong Football
A History

The Hong Kong F.A. was founded in 1914, and came about due to foreigners introducing the sport to the locals. Unfortunately all the early history and records were lost during the Second World War, and the vast majority of such information to that date can only be gleaned from the prolific number of English language Chinese Newspapers of the period.

The mid-19th century saw the British establishing trading links with the Far East by way of trading ports which were situated on the coastline of China, at such places as Shanghai, Singapore and Hong Kong. Eventually foreign settlements were set up in these ports, and the British, together with other nationalities - particularly European - brought with them their pastimes and their sports. As well as tradesmen there were various military establishments, with the outposts being manned by such outfits as the Royal Garrison Artillery (the 'Buffs') and the Royal Navy. Towards the late 19th century, football had become a major sport in Britain, and it was the military that were one of the leaders in the development of the game (notable frequent F.A.Cup Finalists were the Royal Engineers in the early years of this competition). In 1886, the first Hong Kong (and indeed the first in China) organised team was formed, that of the 'Hong Kong Football Club' - although this pioneer was far removed form the current Club that currently exists with that name. The Club was created following a meeting that was held at the Victoria Recreation Gymnasium on the 12th of February. Some football matches had already been played in the Colony - between 'scratch' teams - although these had more of a Rugby bias. The intention was for the Club to play either of the football codes, and five days after the Club's formation, Lieut. Metcalfe's XV met Dr.Thomson's team in a rugby match at the Racecourse. Two days later, the 19th of February, Lawrie's Xl beat Wallace's Xl by 1-0, at the same venue, in the first ever formal Association match in Hong Kong. On the 16th of March, Hong Kong Football Club as such, entertained the Royal Engineers at Happy Valley, the first true match of the new Club. The Hong Kong line-up consisted of:

W.H.Wallace (Captain), G.A.Caldwell, T.Glass, J.Gow, M.D.Griffith, F.Jarvis, C.E.Lawrie, J.H.Stewart-Lockhart, E.Mackean, C.P.Pedlar and A.G.Stephen.

Other football clubs soon appeared on the scene, and as the colony built up in numbers, schools were created, and football soon became part of life for the children of the foreigners. The same development was of course taking place in the other Ports, but Hong Kong was the leader, and in September 1896, the 'Hong Kong Shield' was presented by the community, which was to be competed for annually by the "Military and Civilian Association Football Clubs". HMS Centurion were the first winners, when they beat Kowloon F.C. 2-1. Hong Kong F.C. became the first civilian winners in 1899 - and therefore already the composition of this premier Club must have changed. In February 1906, the first representative match was played by the Colony, when a Hong Kong eleven beat Canton 6-0. Although the Hong Kong F.C. had well established itself, with many members (but poorly attended A.G.M.'s), the military and naval teams tended to operate independently from their civilian counterparts. Clearly a proper organisation was needed, and following a meeting at the YMCA rooms on the 11th of June 1913, under the Chairmanship of Mr.Frank Browne, the Hong Kong F.A. was founded, and in 1914, became affiliated to the Football Association in London.

1913 also saw the first meeting of Hong Kong and Shanghai, for the 'Interport Cup' (a 2-1 victory to Shanghai), in what was to become an annual and keenly competed fixture. The Hong Kong team included players from the Police, the 'Buffs', the Royal Engineers and Hong Kong F.C. It should be noted that until the early 1900's, the game was still very much a foreigner's domain, with little interest expressed (and probably not allowed!) by the indigenous Chinese. However, returning students from Europe and America brought back an interest, together with the youngsters in the Hong Kong schools, and in 1904, the first truly local Club was formed, the South China Athletic Association.

On the 4th of February 1913, the Club represented China in the first Far East Asian Olympic games, which were held in Manila, where they lost 3-1 to the Philippines (the only other football competitors). The South China team was totally composed of indigenous players. The team to represent China in subsequent representative matches was usually chosen following matches between area teams, usually Shanghai and Hong Kong.

In 1923, China were invited to undertake a football tour of Australia, and the selected team showed a predominance of South China players. By now there was a Hong Kong Football League (containing at least two divisions), which was - albeit - dominated by foreigner's teams. However, two indigenous teams were particularly prominent, South China and Kowloon, the latter appearing in seven consecutive finals (up to 1929), of the prestigious 'Hong Kong Shield' Cup Competition. By now, the Chinese had a passion for the game, and the enthusiasm of the fans often reached near riot situations, with the discharging of fireworks during matches, and encroachment on the pitch. Despite the unease and insurrection taking place in China, football continued in the relatively trouble-free Port areas, which tended to be aloof from the enormous changes taking place throughout the countryside.

After South China A.A. were refused permission to postpone their first League match of the 1931/32 season (in order to play a fixture against the touring Malayan Chinese team), the Chinese teams in the League withdrew from their Football Association, and formed their own League competition. But the rift was soon mended, and the locals returned to the parent body in May 1932. China entered the 1936 Olympics football tournament, and the 22 squad players (who were selected following an extensive tour of the Far East), contained a predominance of South China men, plus two 'Athletic' players (a South China offshoot Club). The Games saw the Chinese play in their biggest match, when they faced Great Britain, a game they lost 2-0, but where the team was given much praise by the World Press.

Despite the outbreak of the Second World War, football initially continued as normal, but after the occupation of Hong Kong by the Japanese, the sport all but stopped, until the surrender of the occupying forces in 1945. During the grim Wartime period some interest was maintained via 'mini'soccer'

(presumably 5 or 6-a-side) games. The return of peace to the Colony, allowed the reformation of the local F.A., but under the rather strange name of the 'Fook Hing Rehabilitation Football Association', and at which time Wong Ka-Tsum was elected Chairman (no date has been found for the re-naming of the organisation to the more logical Hong Kong Football Association). During the early part of 1945, just four teams were in formal competition, viz. The Army, The Navy, The Airforce, and Chinese United. No League competition was played, but in addition to a simple 'round robin' tournament, matches were also competed for the Lei Wai Kwok General Cup, and the Law Man Kam Cup.

The first true season - 1945/46 - saw additional teams entering the fray, and at the end of that campaign, the R.A.F. became the Champions of the first post-war League competition, with the '44 Commandos' as runners-up. One year later, more teams entered the League, significantly several with a more local flavour, not least Sing Tao, who topped the final table, with South China in second place. The re-entry of the old established South China Club - who for some months were known as 'Western United' until late 1946 - became a dominant force over the years, with currently over 20 Championships to their credit. Apart from the first season, foreign teams were absent from the major honours lists, and with local interest rapidly re-gaining a foothold, there were soon two divisions, each with at least ten members, although these initially included no fewer than five (British) Army teams. The early post-war years saw the entrance charges to matches varying between $HK 1-20 and 2-40 (in present day terms between about 10 to 20p).

The Senior Shield (knock-out Cup) Competition had also been introduced during the first post-war season, and the initial winners were the Navy 'B' team, with the 1st Commandos as losing finalists. All matches at this time were played on one of four Grounds, those of the Army, the Navy, South China Stadium (which still remains, and is probably much the same today) and Boundary Street Sports Ground (which also still remains, and is very close to the main Stadium at Mong Kok, on Kowloon. By the 1950's, Hong Kong had become the dominant force in Asian football, with match attendances ranging from 7,000 up to a maximum of 28,000, the latter the capacity of the newly instituted Hong Kong Government Stadium.

Pre-war action at the Army and Navy Ground
note the Stand constructed of bamboo.

In the early post-war years, European players were still prominent in Hong Kong

In the 1950's, despite their Amateur status, some players were earning a full monthly wage plus bonuses in football

The post-war Hong Kong F.A. itself started in humble surroundings, by sharing premises with a printing company in Central Prince's Building (the 'office' consisting of just three tables). But in 1953, a move was made to larger premises at the Hong Kong Football Club in Sports Road (near the famous Happy Valley Racecourse) at a monthly rental of $HK 75 (approx. £7), on a 20 year lease. The lease was later extended for a further six years, before the F.A. moved into their own building - which was provided by the Hong Kong Government - on the Kowloon mainland. From an initial number of three staff, this has now risen to around 20. The Hong Kong F.A. Building is a very impressive building, for what can in fairness only be considered a minor football nation.

The new Hong Kong F.A. Headquarters was opened in 1979

Meanwhile on the pitch interest in the game increased to such an extent that in the 1960's it was not unusual to see fans queuing all night for tickets for such encounters when South China played other leading teams. South China's dominance continued, and they were very much a team of locals, with notably Yiu Chak Yin, Wong Chi Keung, Ho Cheung Yau and Mok Chun Wah, who were collectively known as the 'four aces'.

The sport reached its peak in the colony during the 1970's, by which time professional players were common. Professional football was nothing new to Hong Kong, for even in the pre-war days some so-called Amateurs were paid regular wages and received bonuses for playing football. Acknowledged Professionalism rapidly spread throughout the Clubs, and for the 1968/69 season such players were formally recognised by the local F.A. Initially just five teams turned to paid players in their teams, Sing Tao, Kowloon Motor Bus, Yuen Long and Rangers - although only two of these (Sing Tao and Rangers) are still leading Clubs. Between the five, 60 players were registered as professional. The ball had been set rolling by Rangers, who aptly imported a trio from Scotland, namely, Derek Currie, Walter Gerrard and Jackie trainer. The move paid off, for that season the Club came close to winning the 'treble', becoming League Champions, capturing the Senior Shield, and only losing at the final hurdle in the prestigious Viceroy Cup.

Rangers' successes spurred other teams to recruit professionals, and for the 1969/70 season, Caroline Hill, Jardines and Fire Services, joined the ranks.

The boom years:
(top) Crowds packed the Grounds whatever the weather, and (above) fans would queue all night for tickets for the big matches. (left) The players enjoyed a high status - here one sets out to a match by helicopter.

The slump - near empty grounds, and bored fans. But the return of foreign 'imports' in the late 1980's once more increased interest.

The old established South China F.C. were one of the last to turn from amateur status, and of the leading clubs, only Hong Kong Football Club and Police, did not make the change. Further inducements to professionalism were realised when huge sums of money were forthcoming, notably for the newly created Seiko and Bulova clubs, whose parent companies backed them. The quest for honours led to new heights, and such famous English players as George Best, Brian Powell, Kevin Keegan and Mick Channon were eventually to be

enticed to show their skills in Hong Kong. But fast as support was forthcoming, so was a slump that hit the local scene in the early 1980's, and with both Bulova and Seiko ceasing their sponsorship (at the end of the 1985/86 season), football interest in the Colony plunged to an all-time low.

Cash limitations rapidly led to fewer imports, and in addition as so much was being paid to outsiders, there was little left for talented local players. To control the situation, in 1986, a total ban was placed on foreign players.

Inevitably this rapidly led to a further dwindling of interest, and for a while Hong Kong football was at a very low ebb. However, with sponsors once again being attracted, and the ban on foreign players lifted - albeit First Division clubs were only allowed two 'imports' each - support soon rose once again; for the 'Camel Paint Senior Shield' match in December 1989, attracted a near full house. Such a large crowd would have been unthinkable just a couple of years earlier. Near empty stadiums once again began to fill on a regular basis.

Personalities:

Lee Wai Tong was the Colony's greatest local player in the pre-War era, and in the 1950's to early 60's the best known footballer was Yiu Chak Yin. Cheung Chi Doy followed in the path of Yiu, and Wu Kwok Hung became first noticed in 1972. Wu started with the Tung Sing Club as a reserve in the late 60's, and at that time decided he wanted to be a professional. Tung Sing (now in the Third Division) lost him to reigning League Champions South China in 1970, and two years later he moved on to the (now defunct) Seiko team. His stay at Seiko lasted 13 seasons, during which time he picked up nine Championship medals, amongst many other awards, and was first 'capped' for Hongkong in 1973. His illustrious international career continued until 1985, during which time he played over 100 games for the colony. Six times he won the Hongkong player of the year award, and was also voted the best player of the 1980's. Wu finally retired from football in 1986, at the age of 38.

Although unheard of in the World stage, two local players were hugely popular with the fans. Ho Cheung-yau, was a leading player with South China in the 1960's, and he was also renowned for his outstanding fair play both on and off the field. He surprised many followers, when he retired at an early age, in 1969, to take up a career in the Merchant Navy. But one return to Hongkong was a particularly proud moment for him, when he came to collect his M.B.E. (Medal of the British Empire). Ho is now a taxi-driver in Melbourne, Australia. Around the time of Ho's football career twilight, Kwok Ka-ming made his appearance.

Born in Yuen Long, he first played for Rangers, but when that club experienced severe financial difficulties, he was transferred to Caroline Hill. He was soon chosen for the International squad, later became the player/coach of the team, and in 1982 was appointed the National Coach. His abilities did not go unnoticed, for in 1978 he too received the M.B.E., for his contributions to society and local football.

Veronica Chiu: In a male dominated sport it is most unusual for a female to have such a dramatic effect, but Veronica Chiu was an exception. Not only was she the first woman to run a football club in the colony, but she was also instrumental in introducing foreigners to Hong Kong. She became the first individual to own a professional Chinese team, and was also the principal behind the formation of the local women's soccer federation. As a child she was said' to prefer to play football with her brothers rather than play with her dolls! In 1964, together with her husband, she developed an interest in the Yuen Long club, and then moved on to Rangers, Caroline Hill and Sea Bee. Although very wealthy, it was said that she spent over $HK 30 million in the sport. One of her most notable achievements was her saving of Caroline Hill from relegation with her purchase of six Southampton players from England. George Best was another acquisition (for Sea Bee in 1984), and in all she 'purchased' 70 overseas players. By 1993, although well into her sixties, she was now attached to clubs at a lower level, being the Secretary of two Third Division teams (Greatfield and Fishing Boat Sports Club).

(Right) 1993 'Footballer of the Year', Eastern's Lee Kin-wo. (Above) Veronica Chiu.

Principal Post-war Honours:

Season	League Div.1 Champions	Runners-up	F.A.Cup Winners	Runners-up	Senior Shield Winners	Viceroy Cup Winners
1945/46	R.A.F.	Commandos			Navy 'B'	
1946/47	Sing Tao	South China			Sing Tao	
1947/48	Kitchee	Sing Tao			Sing Tao	
1948/49	South China	K.M.B.			South China	
1949/50	Kitchee	K.M.B			Kitchee	
1950/51	South China	K.M.B.			K.M.B.	
1951/52	South China	Army			Sing Tao	
1952/53	South China	Kitchee			Eastern	
1953/54	* K.M.B.	South China			Kitchee	
1954/55	South China	Kitchee			South China	
1955/56	Eastern	South China			Eastern	
1956/57	South China	Kitchee			South China	
1957/58	South China	K.M.B.			South China	
1958/59	South China	K.M.B.			South China	
1959/60	South China	Happy Valley			Kitchee	
1960/61	South China	H.Valley & Tung Wah			South China	
1961/62	South China	Happy Valley			South China	
1962/63	Yuen Long	Tung Wah			Kwong Wah	
1963/64	Kitchee	Happy Valley			Kitchee	
1964/65	Happy Valley	South China			South China	
1965/66	South China	Happy Valley			Rangers	
1966/67	* K.M.B.	South China			Sing Tao	
1967/68	South China	Sing Tao			Yuen Long	(Instigated
1968/69	South China	Sing Tao			Jardine	1969/70)
1969/70	Jardine	Sing Tao			Sing Tao	Jardines
1970/71	Rangers	Jardine			Rangers	Eastern
1971/72	South China	Caroline Hill			South China	South China
1972/73	Seiko	South China			Seiko	Seiko
1973/74	South China	Seiko	(Instigated 1974/75)		Seiko	Rangers
1974/75	Seiko	Happy Valley	Seiko	Rangers	Rangers	Rangers
1975/76	South China	Seiko	Seiko	South China	Seiko	Happy Valley
1976/77	South China	Seiko	Rangers	Tung Sing	Seiko	Caroline Hill
1977/78	South China	Happy Valley	Seiko	Blake Garden	Happy Valley	Seiko
1978/79	Seiko	Happy Valley	Yuen Long	Seiko	Seiko	Seiko
1979/80	Seiko	Happy Valley	Seiko	Bulova	Seiko	South China
1980/81	Seiko	South China	Seiko	Sea Bee	Seiko	Eastern
1981/82	Seiko	Happy Valley	Bulova	Sea Bee	Eastern	Bulova
1982/83	Seiko	Bulova	Bulova	Rangers	Happy Valley	Bulova
1983/84	Seiko	Bulova	Eastern	Zindabad	Bulova	Seiko
1984/85	Seiko	South China	South China	Harps	Seiko	Seiko
1985/86	South China	Happy Valley	Seiko	South China	South China	Seiko
1986/87	South China	Eastern	South China	Happy Valley	Eastern	South China
1987/88	South China	Happy Valley	South China	Tsuen Wan	South China	South China
1988/89	Happy Valley	South China	Lei Sun Flower †	Tsuen Wan	South China	Lei Sun Flower †
1989/90	South China	(Unknown)	(Unknown)	(Unknown)	(Unknown)	(Unknown)
1990/91	South China	(Unknown)	(Unknown)	(Unknown)	(Unknown)	(Unknown)
1991/92	South China	(Unknown)	Borel	(Unknown)	SingTao	Borel
1992/93	Eastern	(Unknown)	Eastern	(Unknown)	Eastern	Eastern

† This is a literal translation of this Club's name, and their present existance cannot be verified.

* Full name 'Kowloon Motor Bus'

As can be seen from the table, Hong Kong football has been dominated by the South China Club, with 25 post-war Championships (from 48), followed by (now defunct) Seiko's 9, and Kitchee with 3. Only 12 different teams have been Champions. Yet the F.A.Cup (which only started in the 1974/75 season), has seen South China as winners on just 3 occasions; with 6 wins, Seiko lead the field. The Senior Shield has produced a bigger variety of winners, including, Navy 'B' (in the first season), Kwong Wah, Sing Tao (three wins), and Yuen Long, each Club claiming their only major achievement. Likewise the Viceroy Cup has a variety of winners (10 in 24 seasons), with Caroline Hill's capture in 1977 being one of the few highlights in their - now past - history; Bulova (winners in 1982 and 1983), together with one senior Shield victory and two League runners-up placings, had precious little to show for the vast sums of money in sponsorship that was put into the team.

Of the 10 teams in the First Division for the 1993/94 season, no fewer than four (Hong Kong F.C., Instant Dict, Kui Tan and Voicelink, have never captured a major honour). Conversely honours' winners, Tung Sing, Blake Garden, and Kwong Wah, now languish in the Third Division. Borel were around for just two seasons, before this company team (it is believed), moved to Macao!

1993/94 Season - Composition of Leagues:

1st Division	2nd Division	3rd Division 'A'	3rd Division 'B'
Eastern A.A.	Five-One-Seven F.C.	A.I.A. F.C.	Greatfield F.C
Hong Kong F.C.	Frankwell H.L.	Citizens A.A.	H.K.Fishing Boat S.A.
Happy Valley A.A.	Fukien A.C.	Golden Sea S.A.	H.K. P.E. Teachers F.A.
Instant Dict F.T.	H.K. Fire Services SWC	H.K.Blake Garden A.A.	Kwong Wah A.A.
Kitchee S.C.	H.K. Police S.A.C.	H.K. Telephone S.& S.A.	Lung Moon S.C.
Kui Tan S.C.	Mansion Holdings Ltd.	Kin. Fruit & V.M.A.	Onclever Limited
Rangers (H.K.) F.C.	Shek Kip Mei S.A.	Martini Sports Club	*G&S Ornament WWG
Sing Tao S.C.	Wong Tai F.& A.C.	Tung Po A.A.	Solon S.A.
South China A.A.		Tung Sing S.C.	St.Josephs F.C.
Voicelink F.C.			Team Fuji Latex F.C.

* Full title "Hong Kong and Kowloon G & S Ornament WWG"

The Grounds in general, and Attendances:

Some appreciation of the size and population spread of Hong Kong is necessary. Hong Kong is situated at the south-eastern tip of China - in size no more than a 'pimple' on an extensive coastline - and adjoins the Chinese province of Guangdong (Canton). This British territory (but only until 1997), consists of Hong Kong Island (78 sq.km.), Kowloon (11 sq.km.), and the New Territories plus outlying Islands (980 sq.km.).

With a population of about 6 million (of whom 98% are Chinese), Hong Kong is a virtual insignificance, both in numbers and size - in comparison to the vast population and area containing China - yet their football ability is on a par with their neighbours (as a comparison England is around 130,000 sq.km. in area with a population of approx. 50 million). The vast majority of the population is squeezed into Hong Kong Island and Kowloom (on the mainland).

The many Islands are sparsely populated, where I was reliably informed that football in any competitive form is not played. The New Territories although by far the largest part of Hong Kong has also only a small population, and although football is played there, it is rare for a senior team to be based in this area of the peninsular. But a team's 'base', is something of an alien term in Hong Kong, for I was also told - with few exceptions - that Clubs do not have 'home' Grounds in the sense that we know them. None the less despite its size, Hong Kong arguably boasts the strongest domestic competition in Asia, due in no small part to the 'imported' professional players. Much of the football activity is centred around the Happy Valley Racecourse area, where there is an enclosed Stadium, and in all at least eight 'Grounds' (most are probably little or no more than pitches), which are frequented by the lower Division Clubs.

Amongst the teaming mass of humanity and built-up areas that are squeezed into just two areas (Hong Kong Island and Kowloon), there are precious few Football Grounds. Therefore most teams play on any one of several Grounds, and 'home' and 'away' fixtures - such as we know them - just do not exist; a fixture is simply 'played'. Two notable exceptions are South China (see later) and, I believe, Happy Valley. Although having a list of all the Senior teams, the only possible indication of a Club's broad area, is the address of the Secretary (which is often a workplace) - and of course is no guarantee of the physical location of that Club. Martini Sports Club (3rd Division) on this basis is the only new New Territories Club. On my limited travels (in the air and on the railway), I had a brief glimpse of four Stadiums, apart from the two viewed in detail.

Attendances vary enormously at matches. As would be expected the level and the relative positions of teams in opposition dictate support. For lower division matches, crowds are counted in no more than hundreds (if that), and 1st Division games average between two and three thousand.

Top clashes can attract between 15,000 and 20,000, and for exceptional encounters, e.g. Internationals and Friendlies versus famous foreign sides, the fixtures are held at the magnificent new 'Hong Kong Stadium' (see later notes). Some crowd figures from the late 1980's suggest these numbers held good then; most First Division games would attract around the 2,000 mark, but this number could vary enormously. In November 1987, a new record low of 250 was recorded for the Sing Tao versus May Ching clash at Mong Kok, and this was 'bettered' when just 145 were present when Sing Tao entertained Po Chai the following May, at the same venue. But that same season, saw an attendance of 17,000 at the Hong Kong Stadium for the virtual Championship decider between Happy Valley and South China, but equally around the same time, at Mong Kok, Sing Tao pulled in only 260, their 1-0 victory over Sea Bee placed them third in the table! Yet in direct contrast, Po Chai Pills and Double Flower (both First Division strugglers) attracted 2,114 at Mong Kok for their dour battle. The Interport match between Hong Kong and Guangdong (Canton) had an attendance of 20,720 in January 1988.

International Football

(N.B. Hong Kong have also appeared under the guise of 'Taiwan' which has been ignored here):

Asia is not known for top level football, nor for support amongst its peoples. However, in the early post-war years, Hong Kong held their own on the Asian international stage. But the World's show-piece, the World (or Jules Rimet) Cup has eluded the Colony, so far as the final stages are concerned. Ironically in modern times, with greater chances of reaching the competition proper, Hong Kong has slipped compared to their contemporaries. Much of their lack of success on the International field has been attributed (at least in the past) to their virtual obsession with success at Club level - with the large quota of foreign players - which stifles the ambitions of local players who if nurtured properly, could probably at least equal the national counterparts of other Asian countries.

Over the years, there have been and still are, a myriad of Asian competitions, and Hong Kong have tried their luck at most of them. The World Cup

was first entered in 1974. That year they won their group 'A'' (sub-group 1) matches in Seoul, then lost 3-1 to South Korea in the semi-finals of group 'A'. On only two other occasions have the team passed the first preliminary stage. In 1978, they topped their group of five, but finished bottom of the next group (of five again). Eight years later the story was similar (first of four, then bottom of two). However, the match that is particularly remembered in the team's history was that played against neighbours China in 1985. In the preliminary sortie, Hong Kong obtained five victories, one draw and no defeats (including wins over Brunei by 8-0 and 5-1). China were also in this group, and after a scoreless draw in Hong Kong, the return match, played in Beijing, was expected to be a formality for the home team. But much to the dismay of the locals in the People's Stadium - which led to riots when the fans displayed their frustration - the Colony pulled off a shock 2-1 victory. However, they later were no match for Japan, losing the 2nd round games, 0-3 and 1-2.

The Asian Cup was first held in Hong Kong in 1956, but as hosts they pulled off no shocks. The tournament was a creation of the Asian Football Confederation (founded in the early 1950's), and the matches, played on a league basis, were well attended at the Government Stadium, with a crowd of 25,000 present for the opener between South Korea and Israel. The post-war Olympic games saw the team first entered in 1984, but they have never gone past the qualifying stage, and they have faired no better in the Asian Games, which are held every four years, never having reached the last four (in 1958 they were losing quarter-finalists). Of the lesser competitions the only real successes have been in the Merdeka Football Tournament. Hong Kong won the competition - eight teams entered - the first year (1957), and the following year came second of five. In 1959, after beating Japan, they finished bottom of the 1st round winners group. In 1970 they came fourth, and one year later - their last in the competition - third.

The Hong Kong team and the fans celebrate after the shock victory over China in May 1985.

At Club level, the Asian Champion Teams' Cup was first held in 1967, when South China lost to Bangkok Bank in the 1st round. During the following few years the Cup was held as a tournament, but there were no Hong Kong entries, and the competition was suspended between 1972 and 1984. On its resumption, Seiko topped their three team group of matches played in Colombo, Sri Lanka, then promptly withdrew from the competition! South China were again the representatives (for the next three years), but made little impression. In the Asian Cup-Winners Cup it has been a similar unsuccessful story - until 1994. By pure luck, whilst in Guilin (China), I was able to see part of the second-leg final of this Cup, when Hong Kong were repre-

sented by - South China. The Islanders lost the first leg at home 4-2, and the return tie - against Al-Qadisiyah of Saudi Arabia - saw the home team win the game (and hence the Cup), by 2-0. The highlights that I saw were quite entertaining, although both defenses, on European standards, were somewhat naive. The attendance totalled some 11,000, consisting of all-white clad Arabs, which produced in the Stadium a bright, if not colourful, view. The dignitaries certainly gave a new meaning to the expression 'corporate hospitality' (or executive boxes), for they were seated on a large platform - shaded from the sun of course - literally in armchairs, and with decorative tables that were laden with refreshments. These spectators certainly seemed to enjoy the proceedings!

The Clubs:

As with any Country, Clubs come and Clubs go, and Hong Kong is no exception. However, here we have a different situation from most others, for in the pre-war days, the game was dominated by foreigners - both clubs and players - from a diverse range of nationalities (both civilian and military). The Chinese gradually began to form an interest, and eventually there were a number of purely indigenous teams.

After the Second World War, for a short period, the sport was dominated once again by foreigners, but this time by British Service teams. After the Chinese had 'taken over' again, a relatively brief period saw vast sums of money in sponsorship, and although many foreigners came to this area of the South China Sea, they were as individuals, and their presence did not affect the actual Clubs themselves, except for those that were formed at that time, and adopted their Sponsors' names.

South China A.A. in its heyday. (back, 3rd left) Yiu Chak Yin, (front, 2nd left) Wong Chi Keung, (front, 3rd left) Ho Cheung Yau and (front, 2nd right) Mok Chun Wah - known as 'The Four Aces'.

South China Athletic Association: During the long history of Hong Kong football this club has dominated, not only with its achievements but for its longevity. The roots of the Club originated in 1904, by students returning from Colleges in Europe and America, who brought back with them a passion for football. The headquarters of the Club was located in the Caroline Hill area of Hong Kong Island, where they are still situated today. Although an Athletic Club by title, football was, and always has been, one of the main diversions. The Club represented the Country (China) in the first ever Far Eastern Asia Olympic Games, in 1913, and two years later they won the football gold medal.

During the pre-war years, they continued to compete also as an area (South China) rather than a Club. Frequent challenges were made with clubs on Mainland China, predominately with Shanghai. After the First World War, the Club was accepted into the European dominated Hong Kong Football Association, although their split personality still allowed them to represent China proper in the local Olympics - which they won again in 1919 - a feat repeated several more times during the ensuing years. In 1923, the Club first captured the First Division title, which had previously been won only by European teams, and this feat was repeated, in 1926, 1931, 1934, 1938 and 1940.

The Club became not only the dominant Chinese team in the colony, but also a regular League and Cup winner amid European football domination.

When the hostilities were over, they took up where they left off, and to this day are by far the most successful (and ethnically oldest) Club in Hong Kong. Yet they remained Amateur for many years  after their contemporaries had adopted professional status. But South China were somewhat sham amateurs, for the players were always assured of good and well paid jobs outside of football. Eventually the Club succumbed to market forces, and formally adopted professionalism in 1980, but it took time before the team regained its former glories, with no major honours between 1981 and 1985, an eternity for such a previously dominant Club. In fact after finishing 7th of 10 (just one point above a relegation place), the following year was the most ignominious. They were wooden-spoonists, two points below the next Club, and it was only due to Second Division Champions (Police) deciding against promotion, that kept South China in the First. South China A.A. are one of the few Clubs who have their own Ground (which is covered later). Currently the Athletic Club has a membership of around 14,000.

Hong Kong Football Club A somewhat grandiose name for a team, but to a degree deserved, for their history goes back to the 19th century, and a club by this name was in fact the first in the Colony. Yet although a dominant pre-war Club they have yet to win a major honour since that time, but there is little doubt that the current Club is totally different from the former. Their Ground is the only one noted on maps as a 'Football Ground' (in Sports Road) rather than a just a 'Stadium'.

Police are another long standing Club, having been around at least since the 1920's (their first First Division Championship was in 1926), however the composition of the teams have radically changed since those days. The Club in the past was predominantly European, but after the War, local Chinese were soon integrated into the Force, and they soon became the players in the team.

The Police are another Club who have made little impact, and in fact are currently in the Second Division (although they were Divisional Champions in 1983 they declined the opportunity of promotion).

St.Josephs are at present only a Third Division team, yet they too are an old established Club. For many years they were composed principally of Portuguese and English Students, but since the 1950's - on the field - they have become just an 'also ran'.

Eastern in contrast have had a good share of post-war success. They were founded in 1927 - their founders being of principally Indian origin. Their good record in pre-war days slumped to a degree after the hostilities, but overall they have over the past 50 years had more than their fair share of honours.

Sing Tao despite the Chinese name were composed of Europeans (all bar one) when they were formed in 1927. It is most likely that they were a mainland China based club, and a totally different organisation from the current one. This supposition is borne out by the fact that they were reformed in the early 1940's, when Aw Hoe (son of millionaire Aw Boon Haw who made his fortune selling 'Tiger Balm') spent a vast fortune on the team. They became the first Hong Kong team to tour England (in the late 1940's), when they played nine matches against Amateur teams in the South. Dominant up to and around the 1970's, it is now some years since they have won a major honour, and in the late 1980's had a spell in the Second Division.

Kitchee were only formed in 1948, and were immediately successful winning the First Division Championship at the end of their first season. They have had their share of successes, but not in recent years, and in the late 1980's in fact dropped down to one of the two Third Divisions.

Kwong Wah were around in the pre-war days, and despite benefitting to a large degree by securing some top Chinese players at the time of the mainland exodus of the late 1940's, they have a largely undistinguished record, and are currently in the Third Division.

Rangers were formed in the late 1960's and won several major honours up to the mid-1970's. They

The once dominant Seiko Club celebrate - but they folded in 1987

are, as the name suggests, a Scottish based Club, having been founded by John Petrie, who started as a clerk on the Docks, but soon made a fortune in the colony. At one time he was the national team manager. Petrie was the first to sign non-Chinese professionals (from Scotland - where else).

Seiko, who played in all dark blue, took the League by storm, but soon disappeared equally as rapidly. Formed by Wong Chong po in 1970), the owner of the famous Seiko watch company, they became League Champions in their debut season, aided in no little part by the vast sums of money invested in the team. Apart from other successes they achieved an

unprecedented record of seven straight championship wins in the 1980's. Their 'star' players came principally from Holland, and amongst their ranks included many former foreign internationals. The last League Championship win was in 1985, foreign professionals were banned, and just a couple of years later (despite winning two major Cups in 1986) they folded.

Bulova had a similar story to tell, (although with a bias towards British imported players), except their's was an even briefer existence. They were only founded in 1981, by Kwong Chong Shan (another famous watchmaker), and also immediately produced successful results, winning not only the F.A.Cup, but also finishing as runners-up in the League on two occasions.

Amongst a galaxy of stars signed by the Club, Charlie George from England was probably the most famous, and also the most unreliable! But after just three - very rewarding - seasons, Bulova threw the towel in, when the F.A. restricted imported players to a maximum of three, the Club feeling that they would lose their prominance with the inevitable lowering of standards that this would create.

Tsuen Wan, were once quite a prominent Club (F.A.Cup and Senior Shield runners-up on four occasions, and 1st Division members in the late 1980's) but they appear to have suddenly vanished. They were one of the rare Senior Clubs that were based in the new Territories, with a 4,000 capacity stadium (and probably played at Tai Hang Tung). They relied principally (probably totally), on local Chinese players. This kept the wages bill down, but no doubt made them uncompetitive compared to their high-spending opponents from further South.

Jardine were another Company team, who took off well. Senior Shield winners at the end of their first season (1969), League runners-up the following, and disbanded a few years later - although the reason for their retirement was allied to a dispute with the F.A.

Caroline Hill (an area near Happy Valley) are a bit of a mystery, some successes in the early 1970's, relegated from the First Division in 1982, played in the Third five years later and now apparently no longer exist. They would have played 'home' matches at South China A.A. or Hong Kong Stadium. **Zindabad**, had a sole major success (F.A.Cup finalists in 1984), but after finishing 7th from 9 in the First Division that year, they folded. **Sea Bee**, were also F.A.Cup-finalists in the early 1980's, narrowly avoided relegation in 1984 (when they finished bottom of the First Division - but were not relegated!), but they too have also disappeared. **Harps** won promotion to the First Division for the 1984/85 season, and went on to the F.A.Cup Final a few months later - but they are no longer in the League. Of the First Division teams in the late 1980's, there appears to be no trace now of **Double Flower, Po Chai Pills** and **May Ching**

Happy Valley have been a dominant Club over the years. They were strong challengers for the title in 1988, Ng Ping-nam (in the air), clashes with South China's Chan Fat-chi.

Amongst the ethnic pre-war teams who are now no longer around, are **Kowloon**, a Chinese team of high standing in the 1920's and 30's. The 1920's also saw the formation of **Athletic**, an off-shoot of South China A.A. The demise of the pre-war European Clubs, who with few exceptions dominated Hong Kong football are now, not surprisingly, no longer around. Such teams as **R.N.Ships, Engineers** (one of the most successful), **Wiltshire Regiment, Navy,** **Combined Services** and **The Welsh Fusiliers,** together with the civilian teams including **Recreation, and Jewish Recreation.** After the Second World War, the immediate successes of **The R.A.F. and The Royal Navy,** were shortlived, although as recently as 1988, **British Forces** were members of the Third Division.

Miscellaneous Jottings:

The magnificent Hong Kong (National) Stadium during construction

In the 1920's some boys were taken to court for causing traffic disruption in a busy street. The policeman told the judge that: *"When I approached the boys, one of them picked up the ball. I cautioned him that it was against the rules"*. *"Of Football?"*, asked the judge. *"No, the traffic rules"*, replied the constable, amongst much laughter in the Court!

The Hong Kong F.A. (founded in 1914), became affiliated to FIFA and the Asian Football Conference in 1954. The national colours are Red Shirts, White Shorts and Red Socks. In 1991, there were 85 registered clubs.

China and Hong Kong before the Second World War were effectively one Country, and although dwarfed by their neighbours, the Colony were more than equal to their neighbours. Each area (Treaty Port) had its own League, although many inter-Province

matches were played, and on the International stage, it was often a Hong Kong X1 under the name of 'China'. However the communist takeover in China in October 1949, led to a definite break between the two (China and Hong Kong). It is only in recent years that the pre-war 'Inter-port' matches (normally between Hong Kong and Shanghai) have been resurrected.

Hong Kong are always pleased to entertain foreign touring sides, and the colony is a popular venue for such teams. Amongst the many visitors, have been Islington Corinthians (a London Amateur side that was touring the World), in 1938. More recently - and just before my visit in April 1994 - the local fans were in good spirits after their victory over Sao Paula of Brazil. In reverse the first foreign tour by Hong Kong (in the guise of 'South China') was made to Australia in the 1920's.

Discipline. The Chinese are no more inscrutable and patient than any other nationality when it comes to football. But suspensions can be very severe. Although a 3 match ban is the norm, it is not unknown for a transgressor to receive a 5 year ban, or even sin die.

The composition of the League consists of 37 teams in 4 different divisions. In the 10 team First Division, nine employ professional players, and even at the lower levels there are over half a dozen with fully paid players, and a few who are semi-pro.

Programme cover for the 1994 'Carlsberg Cup' competition.

although the temperatures were only around the low 20 degrees c., the humidity rose to up to 90% - create your own in-built shower whilst you walk!)

Match programmes are extremely rare. Never are they issued for domestic matches, sometimes for those versus touring sides, but usually a brochure type programme for tournaments. The entrance charges for matches varies greatly, and is dependant on the status of the game, and normally decided by the Clubs themselves. $HK 40 (about £3-20) would be a typical figure.

The youth are the footballers of the future, and although there are few high level clubs in the New Territories - where ironically there is plenty of space for pitches (but few players to fill them and fans to watch) - Clubs for youngsters do exist. At least three from this area were included in the Coca Cola Knock-Out Cup, which had around 15 entrants.

The Hong Kong season extends from September to May or June. There is no ideal time since for much of that period it is not only very hot, but very often extremely humid (during my short visit in April,

Despite few Clubs with their own home Grounds, fans do tend to support specific Clubs, rather than just watch who is playing next at their local Stadium! Some Clubs are franchised, therefore it is possible for the 'local team' to suddenly be based miles away! Football is governed here very much by the '$', with many Clubs being owned by multi-millionaires, who run their team not only altruistically, but also as a business venture. Such interest is valuable to Hong Kong football, and supposedly it is not unheard of for a major team finishing bottom of the League, to have their relegation waived!

A personal experience.

From: Happy Valley

To: Fat Kwong Street

I 'found' two more Hong Kong Grounds, after I had arrived home! For it was only on looking at my camcorder film of our aerial arrival (something of an experience in itself as you appear to land in amongst the skyscrapers on to a narrow runway, with the sea on each side), that I realised I had inadvertently 'taken' two Grounds. After an intensive study of these pictures on still frame, etc., I still don't know what Grounds they were, or even were they are! However, I believe they were taken over the Kowloon peninsular, but neither are the Mon Kok Stadium. One, or both, could possibly be King's Park Sports Ground - which is split into two - if in fact there is a Stadium as such, within, but this is unlikely. Equally, or more likely one could be Boundary Street Sports Ground - this being one of the early post-war venues for football. Intriguing! They could also have been just within the New Territories area. I rather think that they will just have to remain a mystery.

Arriving late afternoon, meant that there were only two clear days left to explore, and since Ground-hopping was not the main reason for our visit, this aspect would have to be fitted as best as could be managed, and within reason. With no knowledge of Hong Kong football (other than the address of the F.A.), I took the opportunity to trace any possible Grounds from several tourist maps that were soon obtained. This opened several possibilities, most of which were situated on Hong Kong Island.

The first day was taken over to purely play the part of a standard tourist. Although I took the opportun-ity to telephone the local F.A. (free local calls) to check their opening times, just before catch-ing the famous 'Star' ferry - several ferries which travel across the harbour from Kowloon to Hong Kong Island. This water taxi ride is said to be the cheapest in the World, the (posh) upper deck costing just under 10p for a 20 minute or so trip! Another boat trip was taken to the small pictur-esque Lamma Island - certainly no evidence of football here - this trip costing all of 30p! On the subject of prices, Hong Kong for cheap cameras, etc. is now a thing of the past - checking out several items, we found they were no cheaper than England!

An alternative ferry took us back to the mainland, and an area named Hung Hom. The attraction here is an incredible department store, completely sur-rounded by tower blocks, but in the authentic shape of an ocean-going liner shape - quite a sight! The next expedition was to find our way back to our Hotel in Cameron Road. Although taxis are quite cheap here, I always feel that this is a sign of defeat - to see something of the real life of a country you have to travel with the locals. We eventually got our bearings, and returned without mishap. Despite what you may be told, there are few locals who speak English, apart from the Hotels and the tourist shops of course. The people are not hostile, but they equally are not that friendly, so you just have to do your best with pointing and sign language, and not expect a lot of help. The evening was spent on more ferries, buses (and the local underground), plus local markets (some of which stay open as long as customers are around).

Day two, and it was back to Hong Kong Island, this time to travel the tram route from West to East (which passed close to the new International Stadium - by shear luck of course!). This is another inexpensive experience not to be missed. The most amazing thing about this journey, of several miles, is the unchanging surroundings. In any towering office block city, you can eventually reach the more restrained suburbs, but not on the bayside of Hong Kong Island.

Although the modern steel, glass and concrete jungle gives way to older buildings, they still tower high above the pavements, and continue to do so until the land runs out. A stop at Causeway Bay on the return allowed us to walk to the new National Stadium - the highlight that my wife Fay was waiting for with keen anticipation! It is quite an art finding your way around with the teeming masses on the pavements and the heavy throng of traffic - but nothing compared to what we were to be faced with in mainland China.

The National Stadium and South China Stadium.

Although land is of course at a premium, it is strange how several grounds used for football should be so close. The South China A.A. Stadium is located less than 1 kilometre from Causeway Bay station (on the main Hennesey Road), in Caroline Hill Road - the name that once bore the name of a First Division club not so many years ago. My request to view the inside of the Stadium was greeted with some surprise, but there were no objections. This Ground, with a capacity of around 14,000, had very much the 'flavour' and character of a typical old fashioned English ground that has all but disappeared in the country of its origin (more's the pity).

The style is hardly surprising since it was no doubt built in the pre-war era when football was dominated on the Island by the ex-patriates. Two covered bench-seated Stands opposed each other down the length of the pitch, and at one end there was a moderately deep open end, also with basic concrete bench seating. At the other end, there is a two-storey building, which I assumed contained the dressing-rooms, indoor facilities, Gymnasium etc. The pitch was surrounded by a running track, and the advertless perimeter wall consisted of an unusual concrete fence. Apart from the surrounding hills and the tower blocks, the one dominant feature was the curving steel outline of the roofs to the new National Stadium.

South China Stadium - looking South-east (Note the National Stadium in the background)

From the North-west:
(Above) The Main Stand (North-east side), and (below) the similar Stand opposite.

It is ironic that the Island's most successful side, and presumably best supported team, with its own ancient Stadium, should be sited no more than a good goalkick from the architectural masterpiece of the new National Stadium - since except for 'big' matches, this arena is not used for football. There is also a close link with England here, since the Stadium is managed by Wembley International (HK) Ltd, and I was fortunate to have a chat with one of those managers. The Stadium was built on the site of the former National Stadium, and took two years to develop. On any standards it is magnificent, and would serve any country as a fitting national venue.

The design (not unlike that of the new Kirklees Stadium used by Huddersfield Town), is particularly striking due to the incredible roofs which cover both sides. These roofs consist of gigantic curved tubular steel beams which are embedded outside the stadium itself and span about 150 metres to provide the front support for an enormous canopy. The graceful curves of the canopy are fixed at the rear to the back of the substantial raised concrete seating structure. Although both ends are open seating, it is refreshing to see a Stadium with so much covered accommodation (75% of its capacity) for spectators, a factor which is often overlooked when comparing the weather protection afforded by British Grounds to the little more than vast open concrete bowls found in many other countries.

Some facts: Each side consists of three tiers and can each accommodate around 10,000, split in total by top and bottom tiers (18,000 each), and middle Executive suite areas for 2,000 each side.

THE HONG KONG STADIUM
WAS DONATED TO THE PEOPLE OF HONG KONG
BY
THE ROYAL HONG KONG JOCKEY CLUB
WORKING WITH THE URBAN COUNCIL

香港大球場乃
英皇御准香港賽馬會
撥款重建
饋贈香港市民並得
市政局玉成其事
立此為記

The complex contains a 400 seater restaurant, changing rooms to serve a maximum of 150 contestants, 54 electronic turnstiles, closed-circuit TV system, and two enormous video screens.

Work started on the redevelopment of the old Government Stadium (a large concrete step-seated bowl, with floodlights but very little cover), in March 1992. It was first used in 1993, before the two roof structures were erected. The first events to take place after (virtual) final completion were held on the 11th of March 1994, when Sao Paula were the football visitors, and during the three day programme Pop Concerts were also held. On my arrival, in mid-April, the finishing touches were still being put to the complex.

Gaining entry could have been difficult, but after persuading the receptionist of my genuine interest, I was given the status of 'temporary worker' in order to get inside!

Having spent longer than expected at the two Stadiums, it was a shame that further explorations could not be made, for there was also Happy Valley.

Different maps tell separate stories, but one indicated another 'Football Stadium' just one kilometre away, North of the famous Racecourse, alongside the aptly named Sports Road, the 'home' of Hong Kong Football Club, and almost certainly that of the Happy Valley Club - three substantial Grounds in an area of about one half a square kilometre! Additionally the maps also showed the Wan Chai alongside Victoria Harbour, and close to Causeway Bay, but this most likely is not used for football.

(Above) The National Stadium looking South.
(Left) A view from outside the Stadium.

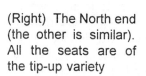

(Right) The North end (the other is similar). All the seats are of the tip-up variety

A mid-afternoon return to the Hotel allowed me time to make my trek to the F.A. (Fay was quite content to have a rest). A study of routes indicated a convenient bus that stopped near the hotel and

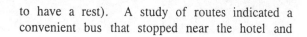

passed quite close (or so it seemed) to Fat Kwong Street - but this particular street was very long, and in a hilly area! With no hope of receiving help in English, getting on the bus presented no problem (the numbers are also displayed in English), but a careful study of the mapping while travelling was necessary in order to alight at the right spot. As my transport turned off Chatham Road North into Wuhu Street, that spot had arrived. I then appreciated that a simple walk on a map is not always the same in reality. After negotiating a complex road interchange, I found Fat Kwong Street, but the F.A.Headquarters were of course at the other end, about one kilometre away, and up a steep hill (on a hot humid day).

The Headquarters are very impressive, and after a wait (I had no appointment), I was served tea, and was most courteously greeted (and not with some surprise) by Vincent Cheung, the Chief Executive Officer of the F.A. An hour long chat - interrupted only by a telephone conversation between my host and Ken Bates who was making arrangements for Chelsea's forthcoming visit - elicited much useful information, plus some souvenirs. My only regret, I found out that there had been a game at Mong Kok Stadium (a bus ride away from the Hotel) the night before, which I could have easily have made! However, a look at two Grounds, and some very useful information, all achieved in two (jet-lagged) days, whilst on holiday, was plenty to be satisfied with. But there was more to come.

The minor Ground taken from the train. (Photo' taken from camcorder 'still').

I toyed with the possibility of an early start the next morning, and giving way to a taxi ride, seek out the Mong Kok Stadium. But discretion won the day, since we were being taken by bus to the Railway Station at 10 a.m. for the trip - and main part of the holiday - into China. I could hardly risk missing this departure. The Railway Station was packed, and everybody seemed to be travelling on our train. As ever I had both the still camera and the camcorder more or less at the ready on the off-chance of seeing something worthwhile. We had barely left the station, before we passed close to Mong Kok Stadium. It was a brief view, no real time to aim either camera, and so my eyes had to be used to provide the images. Mong Kok lies less than 3 kilometres North of the Main Station, to your left, and although I believe it is the principal Football Ground on Kowloon, it was fairly unimpressive. With a capacity around 10,000, it is open on all four sides. Each side is identical, as is each end, and the raised all-seated banks appeared to be in steelwork, and of a temporary type nature (as used as additional Stands at major sporting events), although I have no doubt these were of a permanent nature. In each corner there was a floodlight pylon. Hardly a Ground worth missing the bus for, but I was pleased to have had this brief view at least.

The towering skyscrapers gradually give way to more open vistas, with small towns punctuating the route North. After another brief glimpse of a small Ground as we passed through the Taipo Market area, I decided to have the camcorder absolutely ready for action. My preparations did not go unrewarded, for just a few kilometres further on, a very similar Ground was passed alongside the railway line. This Ground was at Tai Wo (a name that does not feature in the names of the Hong Kong principal teams) and was of an English small non-League club standard. Just open fencing on all four sides, a grass pitch, flat standing all round, and two very small Stands opposite each other. As luck would have it I only managed to get the briefest of shots (15 frames), before a train, travelling in the opposite direction, completely obliterated any further study! And that was it. The end of my personal experiences of Hong Kong football, and so on to China, where investigations were going to be even harder to accomplish.

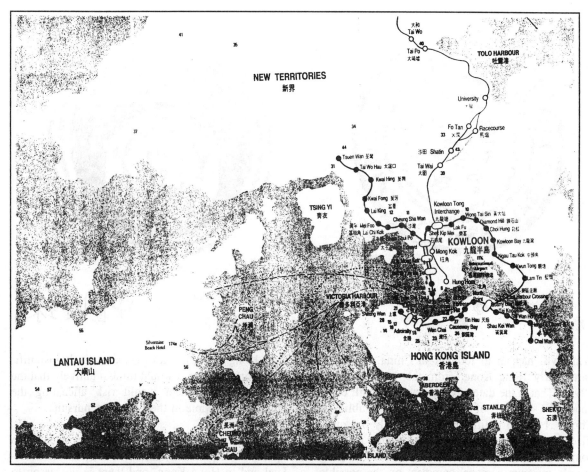

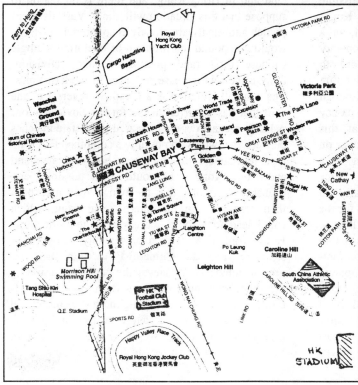

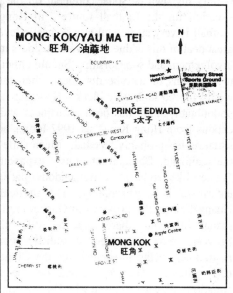

(Top) Map of Hong Kong.
(Above) The Mong Kok Stadium
is off the map to the right.
(Left) Hong Kong Island (North).

1997

and all that.

香港足球總會   中国足球

What will happen to football in China, and more particularly Hong Kong, from the 1st of January 1997? That is the date when Hong Kong will come under the control of The People's Republic of China. I am no politician, and certainly not qualified to comment on the inevitable changes that will come about in Hong Kong. Therefore, the following is only my own personal comment on the possible situation for the football future. In Hong Kong, football is very successful at a domestic level, but a great deal of this is due to private/business monetary involvement and sponsorship. Should either or both these means of income disappear, then the future would indeed look very bleak. However, although undoubtably there has been a business and money exodus from Hong Kong, as 1997 looms near, this situation has probably receded. Meanwhile over on the mainland, China is obviously expanding on a Westernlike style at a tremendous pace. Free enterprise is mushrooming, and particularly in Guangzhou (in the Province of Guangdong), for the casual observer, there appears little difference between the two countries. In addition sponsorship is gradually being integrated into the Chinese football system. Therefore based on the apparent situation, there is no reason why Hong Kong football will not continue in its present form, unless of course, China decides - and is able - to divert some of this money to the mainland. China is a vast country, with Beijing geographically far removed from Hong Kong, and for such a relatively insignificant economic step, I would think it unlikely that the mainland Government would risk alienating the Hong Kong people in their sporting pursuits.

In the pre-War days football leagues were also operated independently of each other, on the Mainland and in Hong Kong, and there is no reason to suppose that this situation will alter. Vast distances (which admittedly are already encountered in China) would compound the problem of operating a single Chinese First (and possibly Second) Division, despite the relative ease of travel in modern times. The football situation is a complete reversal of the split that has occurred in the former Soviet Union. A likely scenario is for increased inter-state matches between the two, with possibly a combined F.A.Cup type tournament that embraces both the mainland and Hong Kong. It would seem possible, and probably desirable, that the two F.A.'s may pool their resources on the International front, which could lead to a more successful united side - the Hong Kong F.A. with a presumably better infrastructure, and the Chinese F.A. with their far greater numbers. Whatever the outcome, assuming that China continues its progression towards 'Westernisation' - without alienating the rest of the World - and their undoubted determination in sporting aspirations, we could see in the not too distant future, a power to be reckoned with in football.

Football in China - A History

Whilst England is the acknowledged founder of the modern game, the honour of inventing football in its broadest sense, is attributed to China. The earliest reference to 'football' comes from the mythical Yellow Emperor of 3,000 B.C., although this is of course not actual fact, there is proof of a 'football' game existing between 300 and 400 B.C. A military textbook, detailing the history of the Han dynasty (206 B.C. to 25 A.D.), refers to military training with the use of 'tsu chu'. Tsu meaning *"to kick with the foot"* and chu, *"the ball made of leather and stuffed"*. There are also other references to a form of football that was played in honour of the Emperor's birthday. On such occasions the 'goal-posts' were hung with decorated silks. As well as the honour of winning, the victors received gifts of wine, fruit and flowers. But the games must have been very competitive, for the hapless losers were flogged and suffered other indignities! In 32 B.C., Emperor Ch'eng Ti remarked that he, together with his soldiers, enjoyed the game: *"We like playing football, and what one chooses to do is not exhausting"*. It is interesting to note that these very earliest references to football, in a military context, can be construed as surviving to this day, with terms that are still used, such as 'defenders', 'attackers', and describing a game as a 'battle'. Perhaps it is little wonder that Wars have been declared over a game of football!

Other descriptions related to this ancient game are very much akin to the modern form, and more so than the earliest evidence of the game in England:

The illustration may be indistinct, but the above is an example (around 300 B.C.) of a game of 'Tsu chu'.

"Eight pointed strips of leather sewn into a ball, filled with air, with roundness an essential to enable it to roll, as well as to fly though the air .... Inflating a football is not easy, for it must not be very hard or it will be too bouncy, nor must it be flabby or the ball will not travel when kicked .... The players form themselves into two parties and the game is decided by points .... Bamboo poles were erected, with a silken net stretched across to form a 'goal' .... in the gaily coloured silks stretched between the poles is an opening, through which the players, in turn, try to kick the ball .... Successful attempts gain points which are scored or recorded .... One of the players acts as the net-keeper and throws the ball back when it fails to go through the hole .... kicking is forbidden under eleven conditions, which constitute fouls. " Whilst such translations may not be precisely literal, the general understanding is remarkably close to today's game. There were ten specified times when football was not played, including: *"On too windy days, when the ground is slippery, after wine, and by candlelight"*. Floodlit football 2,000 years ago!

Therefore when the British brought football to Shanghai in the 19th century, they were no more than re-introducing a game, which had been played by the locals some 2,000 years earlier. European trading with China had existed for several hundred years, but the importation of Opium from India, led to the four Opium Wars (1839 to 1860). Defeat for the Chinese led to treaties which gave Britain access to five treaty ports, plus the founding of an embassy in the 'Forbidden City' of Peking (Beijing). Whereas Britain can be accused of marauding colonisation in this period, they were also responsible for the construction of railways, communications and industrialisation in China. In a totally alien area, Westernisation gradually, and often grudgingly, came.

Shanghai became the first British development - taken by them in 1842 - and was an international settlement in 1863, the 'Hong Kong' of that era. £400m. was invested in turning the area from a humid swamp into the principal industrial city of the Orient. Messrs. Jardine Mathieson & Co. (tea and opium traders) who owned much of the land built the first railway - from Shanghai to Woosung (probably the current 'Wuhan', a City about 600 kilometres East of Shanghai, on the Yangtse River). Shanghai became a centre for World trade, where Westerners (who by the 1920's numbered some 60,000) were able to live in an atmosphere of 'home from home', and where they introduced their own games and sports. The international settlement became a virtual country within a country, which was governed and subjected to its own (Western) laws. The progressive elements in Chinese Society, the elite businessmen, were welcomed into this domain, together with their families, and soon an even greater international atmosphere pervaded within the area. However, outside these confines it was a very different story, where some two million Chinese existed in abject poverty - and it later became the natural breeding ground for revolution.

The first football matches were introduced into Shanghai (and later other areas such as Canton, Hong Kong and Singapore), by visiting ships of the Royal Navy. Around the late 1840's several sports clubs were formed, principally for cricketers, horsemen and rowers, but in 1879 the first organised football match was played between the Shanghai Athletic Club and The Engineers, and this fixture became an annual event. Glaswegian John Prentice, President of The Engineers, was a leading promoter of the game, but it was not until November 1887 that a true Football Club was formed. At a meeting at the Gymnasium, the leading football followers met under the Chairmanship of H.G.Harwood. Two committees were formed, one for Association, and the other for Rugby Football. The previous year, it was reported, 13 matches had been played, but with only one under Rugby rules. At this meeting the first steps were taken to form an independent Football Club, when it was recorded that "... *any man can become a member of the Football Club without being a member of the Shanghai Athletic Club by paying a $5 fee"*. The Club colours were given as amber and yellow. In March 1888, the first true Club game was played, when Shanghai F.C. beat the Royal Engineers 2-0, with the following team: F.Abott, F.P.Catterall, G.A.Matthews, L.Hallward, J.Saunders, R.J.Harris, E.B.Skottowe, E.P.Wickham, W.Bruce-Robertson (captain), A.J.H.Moule and E.C.Pearce. Pearce, at the end of his playing career, was also the Club president, and Bruce-Robertson had been one of the founding-members of Hong Kong F.C. This fixture continued as an annual event, and in 1891, John Prentice (of The Engineers), presented a trophy, to be held by the victors for one year.

The Shanghai Recreation Club was founded on the 9th June 1888, and they used the grounds of the Athletic Club for their matches, a venue that was first used by the, 1863 founded, Baseball Club. This second Football Club was first known as the Rangers, but later changed their title to 'Recreation'. Many Clubs sprang up, some of which soon suffered an early demise - such as Dock F.C. and the YMCA - but amongst the forerunners was an official football section from Shanghai Recreation (in 1902), who became known as 'Shanghai F.C.' This Club soon became the most prominent in the area. In 1902, E.B.Skottowe presented a trophy which was named after himself, and Shanghai F.C. won the first seven finals and also in 1912. 'A' Company Shanghai Volunteer Corps were successful in 1908. 1909 and 1911, and in the other years, Recreation were the winners.

The first League was created in 1907, and Thomas Dewar (the Whisky Company) provided a shield for the Winners. The 1907/08 members consisted of Shanghai Football Club (inevitable Champions), Navy (runners-up), Police, Shanghai Recreation Club, Deluge Co., 'A' Company Shanghai Volunteer Corps, and Engineers - the wooden-spoonists in the seven team competition. John Prentice retained his football prominence, for he was elected president of the League Committee. The Recreation Club soon took over the mantle, from Shanghai F.C., as the best Club for they were the League Champions for the next seven years (up to World War 1). Prentice and Skottowe created the annual International Cup, which was played over the New Year Holiday, (in 1907 for the first time), when local inhabitants formed representative teams, initially from England, Ireland and Scotland (but later joined by other Foreign XI's). John Scott from Greenock founded the Engineers Charity Cup in 1909, for the Champions versus the Rest of the League fixture, with the proceeds going to Chinese hospitals and schools.

Although football was dominated by the British expatriates, other nationalities also joined in, notably the Portuguese, who formed their own Army Club (in 1906), and later 'Recreio Clube' (Recreation Club). In September 1910, the committees of the League, plus those of the Skottowe and International Cups met to form the Shanghai Football Association, which soon became affiliated to the F.A. in London. Sadly E.B.Skottowe, one of the great supporters of the game in Shanghai, died just before the formation of the local F.A., and was therefore unable to see the fruits of his labours.

January 1912, saw the first Shanghai representative match, when a visiting team from Japan was beaten 5-1, and in another match the powerful Recreation Club beat the tourists 1-0. One year later, in February, the first Interport Cup game took place, when Shanghai travelled to Hong Kong, and the visitors won 2-1. The Shanghai team was made up of players from Recreation, Shanghai F.C., 'A' Company Volunteer Corps, Police, and B.A.T.

Undoubtably Shanghai was the leader of football in mainland China, but not surprisingly other Clubs and then Associations sprung up in the other ports. Tientsin (now known as Tientjin), about 150 kilometres East of Beijing, was typical. The first team, Tientsin Association Football Club, was followed by Queens and St.Louis, plus other nationality teams, notably those from White Russia who had fled from the Revolution in their country. Chefoo - renamed Yantai meaning 'Smoke Terrace' (due to beacon fires that were lit on the cliffs to warn the local fishermen of the approach of British ships during the opium wars) had its followers. This (now fairly insignificant) town lies on the Shandong peninsular (East of Beijing), and formed a Collegiate team which toured Shanghai as early as 1890. At the treaty port of Chinkiang (near inland Nanjing) on the Yangtse River, two of the town's main representatives were the Imperial Maritime Customs Club and

Recreation. Recreation was the pioneer Club, and their Ground - Victoria Park - was built in 1897 in honour of the sovereign's silver jubilee.

Canton, in modern day China the leading Westernised province, also had a treaty port, but they like many others had difficulties in arranging matches. These ports were often sparsely European populated enclaves, and were usually surrounded by a hostile indigenous population, at a time of great unrest in China. But collectively they helped to spread 'the word', for until the 20th century, the Chinese expressed no interest in football, seeing any sport as childish and undignified.

Early in the 20th century football and other sports were included in the curriculum of the Schools which had sprung up for the children of the Chinese elite. A situation, not dissimilar from the spread of football in mid to late 19th century England where privileged students of Public Schools took the game back to the working class workforce in the North. Soochow (now Suzhou) University was one of the leaders, forming the East China Intercollegiate Athletic Association on the 3rd of April 1904. Suzhou - one of China's oldest continuously inhabited towns - is now virtually a suburb of Shanghai. Another early ethnic Club was Ching Hua F.C. which was founded at Mei Hsien, in the Kwangtung (Guangdong - Canton) province in 1909. In the more remote areas, the YMCA also helped to spread this particular gospel.

But it was still Shanghai (in the North) and Hong Kong (in the South) where the main influences were exerted. Football amongst the locals was actively encouraged by the foreigners, and in 1909, the YMCA Missionary School and College of Shanghai built a Ground at Hongkew for its Chinese members. The construction of the railways also played a large part in football awareness, and teams sprang up from these companies. The Shanghai-Nanking (Railway) amongst others had good teams, and although initially members came from the British workforce, the local Chinese eventually became interested and then took an active part.

The first real local recognition of Western-type sports was seen in October 1910, when a National Athletic Games was held as part of an exhibition at Nanking (Nanjing). The country was regionalised for qualifying contests.

The Hongkew ground was opened with the staging of the Shanghai trials, and a squad of 40 travelled to Nanking. The games were a great success, and St.John's University of Shanghai won most of the medals.

January 1913, was a milestone in local football, when China made its debut in the Shanghai International Cup, beating Ireland 9-2, although on this occasion the 'China' team was no more than local born sons of Europeans. But on the 4th of February of that year, a true Chinese team (albeit South China A.A.in total) attended the Far East Asian Olympic Games, where they lost 1-3 to the only other football competitors from the Philippines. The political situation construed to suppress local development, for whilst an impression of normality continued in the European enclaves - and football matches continued unabated - elsewhere insurrection was in the air. For the ordinary indigenous population, the sport was virtually unknown, and the Chinese interest extended only as far as the students, with the inauguration of the Inter-collegiate Tournament in early 1912. Nanyang College was the first winner, and they continued to dominate this competition in the early years, when large crowds attended the matches - 8,000 for the December 1914 decider. A further step towards local participation came in that Winter, when the Managing Director of the Shanghai-Nanking Railway donated a Cup, which was to be contested between Chinese workers' teams - the Shanghai-Hanchow-Ningpo XI were the first winners.

South China A.A. from Hong Kong continued to represent the Chinese nation at International level, after play-offs with other regions, but in 1923 a truly representative team undertook a tour of Australia. Although South China still dominated the team members, three other inclusions were Shen Kuo Chuen - the giant Nanyang University forward, plus Wang Chen Sheng and Chang Hsi En who both came from Fuh Tan University. By now suggestions were first mooted that Chinese teams be allowed in the Shanghai League, but after the leading Club, Shanghai College, lost to the European Shanghai Football Club 9-0 in 1924, and a year later Nanyang were thrashed 6-1, such a move would have been premature. But Chinese Sport was given a lift with the formation of the China National Amateur Athletic Federation in Nanking in 1924.

(Left) Captain and goalkeeper Leung Yuk Tong (from the South China Club), and (right) 6 foot high Shen Kuo Chuen (Nanyang University) were two of the players who played in the 1923 Australian tour team.

That year local businessmen formed their own 'Hongs Chinese Football League', for teams comprising of their workers. Customs Club were the first Champions, and received a trophy presented by *Nestle*. The following season the Athletic Federation took over the running of the competition. Unfortunately this came at a particularly anti-foreigner period, and at the Central Chinese Sports Games the cry of *"fan fan"* ('fight') was prominently heard.

Chinese Clubs Tung Wen and Union made applications to join the Shanghai League in 1925, but were turned down, being told that they must first have their own Grounds. Meanwhile Hong Kong were leading the way in acceptance of the Chinese, both in respect of Officials and Clubs. But the (Chinese) Shanghai League continued, Shanghai taking the Championship in 1925, followed by Union the next year. A combination of Shanghai and Hong Kong players played Shanghai Interport that year and

Another tour was made to Australia in May 1927

IN TRAINING COSTUME AT THE SHOWGROUND YESTERDAY
Top row (reading from left to right): Y. T. Leung, S. W. Wong, K. S. Tso, Lau Kan, K. P. Kwok, W. H. Pang, T. S. Lee, C. W. Chen.
Centre row: Y. T. Lai, C. Y. Woo (assistant manager), Prof. K. L. Kwong (manager), Leslie Kwong, W. T. Lee.
Front row: K. C. Fung, K. T. Mak, H. H. Chou, K. I. Chan.

before a crowd of 8,000 lost 5-0, showing that they were still not capable of worthy integration, but Chinese support for the game had reached a level of fanaticism, both vocally and in numbers. In 'China's' 2-2 draw with 'Scotland' in the International Cup, a record crowd of 9,000 was present, and the 4-0 replay defeat attracted 10,000 to the Pioneer Field Ground in Shanghai.

At last the Chinese wish was granted, and in the 1926/27 season, the Three Cultures Club - a truly Chinese team - made its debut in the Shanghai League. The first game resulted in a 3-1 victory over Artillery, followed by a 5-1 win over the Engineers. The newcomers, in green and yellow, were represented by: Hoh, Feng, Chu, Mao, Wong, Wu, Sze, Chang, T.M.Lee, Lee Wai Koon, and Tsao. But the season turned sour, with some heavy defeats, and finally to their disgrace, riots broke out at the Pioneer field in the Charity Cup match with the Engineers. This led to the Club's suspension, but the team, also entered in the Chinese League, ended as runners-up to Loh Hwa.

On a national basis the game had taken a hold, Peking boasted a membership of 22,000 students who played the game, with the Pei Ning - Railway - Team leading the way at Club level. Police were the leading Cantonese team, whilst King Hua led the way in Nanking (then the capital), and Chung Hua in Tientsin. The 1928/29 season saw the entries of Loh Hwa and Union at last into the (European) Shanghai League. The former Club's appearance was fully justified, as they easily won the First Division Championship at their first attempt.

The newcomers also accomplished the 'double' with their victory - 2-1 over the Navy - in the inaugural Shanghai F.A.Cup. But the Chinese Club's excitable supporters brought shame on the Club when they gatecrashed a match which resulted in many injuries. The following season another incident occurred when those 'fans' attacked the Referee after their 4-0 defeat to the Wiltshire Regiment. The Army team had resorted to physical tactics that had angered the Chinese fans (and - according to the local Press - they played into the hands of the Nationalist agitators that were present).

First Division

	P	W	L	D	F	A	Pts
Loh Hwa	10	8	0	2	42	13	16
S.R.C.	11	8	1	2	45	19	16
Police	10	6	4	0	62	22	12
Scots Guards	11	6	5	0	33	29	12
S.F.C.	8	5	2	1	27	20	11
Northants	9	5	4	0	43	26	10
P.S.A.	8	3	5	1	17	41	6
Navy	7	1	6	0	11	31	3
Suffolks	8	1	7	0	19	38	2
Norfolks	7	0	7	0	8	41	0

Second Division "A"

	P	W	L	D	F	A	Pts
Police	9	8	0	1	50	13	17
S.R.C.	8	7	1	0	25	13	14
R.A.M.C.	9	5	3	1	22	19	11
Navy	8	5	3	0	18	15	10
S.F.C.	8	5	3	0	30	15	10
H.Q.N.C.C.	9	4	5	0	22	23	8
3 Cultures	7	3	4	0	22	22	6
St. Xaviers'	9	3	6	0	30	43	6
Erin Villa	7	1	6	0	13	26	2
P.S.A.	7	1	6	0	15	42	2
Deutscher	7	1	6	0	3	24	2

Second Division "B"

	P	W	L	D	F	A	Pts
Signals	8	8	0	0	43	4	16
R.A.O.C.	8	6	2	0	39	17	12
Details	7	5	2	0	34	9	10
Bramtoco	8	5	3	0	24	16	10
12th M.T. Co.	6	3	2	1	14	9	7
St. Xaviers'	7	3	4	0	35	25	6
J.R.C.	6	3	3	0	15	17	6
Erin Villa	7	1	6	0	7	22	2
Tung Wen	8	1	7	0	7	23	2
Pagoda	7	0	6	1	11	53	1

Shanghai League tables during the 1929 season.

The subsequent enquiry put the Chinese at fault, and despite challenging for the title, Loh Hwa resigned; Recreation won the Championship for the twelfth time. But Loh Hwa did not cease playing, for they represented East China and easily overcame their opponents from the North, and took the National Championship Trophy, that had been donated by General Shang Chen.

The North of the Country also had its own competition - the Tiensin League, in which Tiensin A.F.C. and the Army dominated, and in 1930 they joined Shanghai and Hong Kong in the annual Interport competition.

The volatile Chinese - at least as far as football was concerned - continued to cause trouble. A referee was attacked at a Nanking match, and during a tour of the Philippines by the Chinan Institute, 400 of the local Chinese invaded the pitch during a game. But more encouraging was the acceptance of the China National Athletic Federation into FIFA in 1931, and they undertook to build a 100,000 capacity Stadium in the Capital, Nanking. The Football Association, which embraced the F.A.'s of Shanghai, Singapore, Hong Kong and - its latest member - Tiensing, was at that time independent of this Federation.

The Sino-Japanese War in 1932 caused further turmoil in the Country, and the Chinese Clubs had to cease operations, yet in the Ports, life amazingly went on very much as usual. However once Chinese football normality ruled again, the North could be seen to be rising in stature, with such Clubs as Chung Hwa, Nan Min plus the University teams of Peining (from Tientsin) and Peking's Yenching. The sport had by now become popular in Peking, and in 1935, a crowd of locals which totalled 3,000, was present to see their Fu Jen favourites beat the touring team from Tiensin. Shanghai still led the way, in ability and enthusiasm, and when the 1935 National Games were held at the New Civic Centre, in Kiangwan, an incredible crowd numbering 90,000 saw Hong Kong beat Canton. The mid-1930's saw the move of the Shanghai F.A. Headquarters from the Pioneer Field to a new Ground in Yenping Road, and at that time the indigenous Clubs rose from 12 to 28 in number.

China entered the 1936 Olympics Football Tournament, but it was the South China Club of Hong Kong that dominated the squad, with just three players coming from the Three Cultures and Tung Hwa mainland teams. Around that time a touring team came from North Korea, and together with North China each played matches in Shanghai against East China.

A notable member of the North's team was 25 year-old Lee Feng Lu, who had graduated from Fu Jen University, Peking. After the Second World War he was to coach both the People's Liberation Army team plus the National team, and in 1956 he became Vice-President and later President of the Chinese Football Association.

As War approached in England, Japan was still in conflict with China, yet amazingly despite fierce fighting in Shanghai - where the majority of the Chinese armoury and personnel were wiped out - life in the treaty port enclave continued much as usual. But for the local population there were more important things than sport, and football as it was then, was soon to close, and would never be the same again. The Japanese who by now occupied the Capital, Nanking, set-up the 'New China Athletic Association', and in the Winter of 1938, Chinese, but much-changed sides, re-appeared once again in the Shanghai League. The Japanese organised the East Asian Games, and although there were representative teams, including China, the tournament was little more than a sham.

1945 saw a football re-birth, particularly in Shanghai - under the auspices of the Shanghai Athletic Association, but Tung Hwa and Zi Wei were the only Chinese teams to initially accept the invitation to join the new set-up. On the 1st of January 1946, the new League got underway which by then consisted of the following Clubs: Union, Korean SC (the two meeting in the first match which ended 2-2), Tung Hwa, Tsong Peh (a newly formed Club), plus European teams Sokol, Italiano and Jewish Recreation. But it was not long before the non-Chinese broke away, and together with other pre-War Clubs formed their own International Soccer League. In the Shanghai Chinese League, the newcomers Tsing Peh took the title, and also won the Mayor's Cup, the renamed - pre-War - Skottowe Cup, which had first been competed for in 1902.

With drastic political change in the air, the first post-war National Athletic Meeting, in Shanghai, took place in 1948, but several games were played in distinctly unsporting fashion, generally with dissent - and violence - towards the officials. Political ideology was used to the full in the name of football. The 1948/49 season saw Tung Hwa resign from the League after their player - Bob Honniball - refused to leave the pitch after being sent off for striking the Referee; the Ref. walked off instead! A replacement Official took control, and in the 88th minute, Honniball was once again 'sent off', and refused to walk - again. The match was abandoned, the Trophy (The Mayor's Cup), awarded to Tsing Peh, Honniball received a three year ban, and Tung Hwa resigned. The seriousness of football had certainly taken a hold in China! Meanwhile the Nationalists and Communists were battling it out to decide who would run the country, and what was to become, at the end of the 1948/49 season, the last League Championship in Shanghai went to Tsing Peh once again.

The Communists won the more significant battle, and with a mass exodus to Hong Kong, Taiwan, Europe and the U.S.A., so too were included many of the Country's leading players. Under the doctrine of Mao Tse Tung, sport became an important part of the new philosophy, and all forms, including football, came under the auspices of the All China Athletic Federation. The majority of the pre-Communist Clubs disappeared, to be replaced notably by various teams representing the People's Liberation Army.

The Football Federation was reformed, and the initial League Championship, for the first time a National competition, was played in 1951. The majority of the 'Clubs' were Army garrisons in the larger towns and cities. Often teams represented regions rather than the towns themselves, and the first Champions were 'North East' - Bei Tung. This team supplied ten of the Army team that later played in Czechoslovakia, where their inexperience told, when they lost to Dukla Prague by 17-1 and later to CWKS Warsaw 9-1.

In order to prepare for the 1952 Olympics there was no National Championship, instead the prospective Chinese squad played many matches against Town and Regional XI's. Political differences resulted in the Chinese delegation arriving too late in Finland for the Olympics, but the football team played a number of Friendly games, losing to the host Country (4-0) plus three matches in Poland.

1953 saw a re-organisation of football, when leading players from Works, Schools and University teams were sent to the newly founded Sports Institutes, this raised the standard of play, as did the instigation of a National Class 'A' Tournament. The four winning teams played-off the Finals in well-attended matches in Shanghai, and Ba Yi won the title. This form of competition continued for some years, whilst the Country tried to build a strong national team. Between 1954 and 1957, China played 166 games, of which 49 were won and 91 were lost - opposition coming from other Communist country Clubs or Regional XI's, the sole exception being FC Liegois of Belgium. Political differences again prevented China from entering the 1958 Olympics, when they refused to acknowledge the entry of Taiwan.

Amongst the National XI's 70 games played in 1957, was their first match (and final total of three) in the World Cup. Home victories by both China and Indonesia resulted in a Rangoon (Burma) play-off, which ended in a scoreless draw, but progress for their opponents who had the better goal difference from the earlier games. Withdrawal from FIFA came in August 1958 over their objections to the acceptance of Taiwan, but a prolification of International matches continued (237 between 1958 and 1961), with a variety of opponents, including tournaments with other like-minded ideology Nations and touring teams to China from Africa.

Despite their normal lack of 'quality' opposition, the Nation's football ability was improving, but the 'Cultural Revolution' in the mid-1960's resulted in the banning of all competitive sports between 1966 and 1972. However, in 1971 the first tentative steps where taken with national and representative visits to like-minded Countries, as the extremes in the political set-up eased a degree.

INTERNATIONAL FOOTBALL

NEW ZEALAND

VERSUS PEOPLES REPUBLIC OF

CHINA

WEDNESDAY 23rd JULY 1975 — BASIN RESERVE WELLINGTON

OFFICIAL PROGRAMME 40c

(Top) China adventure abroad again in 1975. (Below) Henry Fok who did so much for Chinese football.

With the support of FIFA executive Henry Fok (the anachronistic 'socialist millionaire' Hong Kong XI resident), China were allowed to enter the 1974 Asian Games, where an ageing 'politically correct' team were not disgraced. Further promptings allowed FIFA member Countries to compete with the Chinese, with Mr Fok's support, who enlisted the aid of the Arabs in his attempts to not only ban Taiwan, but also Israel from the World Footballing body.

The 1970's saw countless 'International' matches being played once again, but significantly with a greater proportion of non-Communist opponents.

The Asian Football Conference (of which Henry Fok was Vice-President) admitted China in 1976, and also expelled Taiwan and Israel! In the Asian Cup that year China finished a creditable third. For the next few years, starting in 1977, they welcomed guest teams to China that would earlier have been unthinkable, including New York Cosmos (and Pele) and the West German Amateur team. Perhaps even more remarkable, the Chinese National team toured the USA in October 1977, before 'back home', West Bromwich Albion became the first post-War English team to be invited to Peking and Shanghai. Further guests arrived in China, and other tours were made not only to South America, but also to Britain (in 1979), when matches were played against West Bromwich, Middlesbrough, Chelsea and Celtic. Over this period a staggering number of teams from 29 countries came to China, and in return they visited no fewer than 47!

The political correctness period, followed by the vast number of Representative and National games hardly provided the chance for 'Club' sides to compete in competition, although unofficial matches were played, for the enthusiasm of the game, was difficult to suppress completely. But eventually an official domestic Championship was played in 1973, when Beijing were the winners.

The early years of the new League Championship saw Beijing and Ba Yi (also based in the new capital) as the most successful teams, each winning a hat-trick of Championships. 1980 saw China fully accepted into the International arena with membership of FIFA once again, and that year they were involved in the World Cup, the Olympics and the Asian Cup qualifying matches. But the team, still showing inexperience, managed to reach the finals of only the latter competition.

West Bromwich were visitors to Beijing in the late 1970's, where they played before huge crowds.

West Brom defence thwart an attack from the Chinese.

For the likes of China, qualification for the World Cup Finals is a long and arduous route. Successes against Hong Kong, Macao and Japan, followed by a 4-2 victory over North Korea in the Final of their group, gained them entry into the final group round of the Asia Oceania grouping. A crowd of 80,000 at the Worker's Stadium in Beijing, saw New Zealand hold their hosts to a scoreless draw in a physical match, and then win the return 1-0. Victories over Kuwait and Saudi Arabia, resulted in China having a final play-off match against New Zealand in Singapore. Just one step away from the finals in Spain, they lost this match 2-1.

Some of the Chinese players had by now become noted outside the Country, and in the build-up for the next trio of International Cups, Gu Guangming, in 1984, nearly made a move to the West - to Hamburger SV in Germany - in what would have been China's first such 'export'. On the World Cup front the team had no success, and a highly embarrassing 2-0 defeat at the hands of Liechtenstein (population of around 27,000 compared to China's 1,000 million!) in a Friendly match, became the first official Friendly game at International level played against a Western Country.

The domestic competition still took very much second place to the National team's progress, and also the irregular National Athletic's Meetings, which in 1983 caused the postponement of the League Championship. Instead elimination contests produced eight teams who played a knock-out tournament at the Kiangwan Civic centre, which saw Shanghai defeat the Guangdong provincial team by 5-4 on penalties, before a crowd of 50,000. By now

there were three Divisions operating in China (although it is not clear if these were all on a nation-wide basis, which would seem unlikely for a Third Division in such a vast Country), and a new overall Championship system was devised for 1984. A three week long tournament was held in Wuhan - in central China and approximately equidistant between the four largest Cities - to decide the overall Champions. Seventeen Division 1 clubs, 6 Division 2 plus the 3rd Division Champions competed, and the World Cup style competition was won by Beijing.

Success came in the next Asian Games, although China lost in the Final to Saudi Arabia, but the 1986 World Cup qualifying matches resulted in shame. In order to reach the final qualifying round, a point was needed in the last game, in Beijing, against Hong Kong. Rather than consolidate their position the host team decided to qualify in style and go for a victory. But Hong Kong had other ideas, and after securing a surprise 2-1 victory, the local fans vented their anger with riots, the likes of which had never been seen (following a football match) before. This unacceptable shock result resulted in the resignation of coach Zeng Xueling. Various ideas were tried in order to raise the game in the Country. Two National teams were formed, the 'Yellow' XI being the current champions who played the 'Reds', and later the 'Yellows' (effectively the National 'B' team) were composed of the National Youth team. Drawn matches were not allowed in League matches, and for such results the winners were decided on penalties! In 1987, the overall Champions were again decided on knock-out basis, this time between 12 finalists, and the provincial

October 1985 saw the inroduction of the first F.A.Cup type knock-out competition, which was played in Wuhan.

Shanghai and Shandong (in white) players tussle for the ball.

Guangdong team triumphed. That year it was also decided to allow former National Team players from abroad, who were aged over 28 years, to play in China, and also for Chinese players to 'guest' with foreign Clubs, with hopes that this double-edge agreement would provide valuable international experience.

The experiment seemed to work, for China surged through their 1988 Asian Championship qualifying group, only to disappoint in the Seoul-finals, against more experienced European 'Amateurs'. With such a vast population to call upon, a keen interest in football amongst its people, and a determination to succeed, the overall lack of success led to great frustration amongst the administrators and followers.

The Worker's Stadium in Beijing was one of four venues for the 1985 FIFA Under-16 tournament.

Action from a League match in 1986, between Beijing and Shaanxi.
Beijing's Li Hui scores with a header - in a season criticised for its lack of goals.

At last the late 1980's saw the inevitable - professional football. With the gradual introduction of private enterprise into the Country, came industry leaders and owners who were willing to put money into football - for their own satisfaction and for the publicity of their organisation, i.e. Sponsors. Zhang Furu, the managing-director of the Yuezong Printing Corporation, plus several other business associates created a new Club - Foshan - which was composed of experienced ex-Club players. Foshan is a relatively small City (population of around 200,000), and is better known as being a folk craft centre, but more significantly it is in the Guangdong province, i.e. Canton, the area in which free-trade has been at the forefront in the new 'Cultural Revolution' since the late 1980's.

In the North-east (250 kilometres from Beijing), Mr. Wan Jiachun created the first privately sponsored team, appropriately named 'Wan Chengde' (the family name comes first in China). Initially these two teams were only allowed to play friendly matches, but eventually Fushan were the first such Club allowed into the League. Leading team,

Liaoning, became the first well established Club to employ professionals, and the final commercial acceptance came when the Qixin Pharmaceutical Company sponsored the National team.

More action, this time in a
match with Hong Kong in 1988.

The 1990 World Cup qualifying match with Iran.

The fans go wild in Shenyang after their team's surpise victory.

The National team failed again in the qualifying matches for the 1990 World Cup, but China was given the honour of staging the Asian Games in 1990, despite the horrors of 'Tianamin Square'. There were high hopes of winning the football tournament, and great preparations were made to provide a showpiece tournament. A complex of Stadiums in the North of Beijing were principally used, but the final - at the Worker's Stadium - before an attendance of 70,000 was noted for its absence of the host country, who had lost 1-0 in the quarter-finals to Thailand.

This defeat - before a live crowd of 72,000 and an estimated 300 million TV audience - once again led to frustrating demonstrations (this time more subdued).

These frustrations must be difficult to bear in the largest populated country in the World, for despite its 'Third World' image, it recognises the value and prestige of having a successful sporting pedigree (as has been seen in the early 1990's in other sports). The vastness of the Country hinders progress, but as Westernised practises are accepted, and communication and travel become easier, then more interchanging of players between Clubs, with financial incentives, will no doubt lift the Country's role on the World football stage. In the 1980's a desire to host

the 2002 World Cup has been expressed, and although Japan is also making a strong bid, such an honour would provide an enormous fillip to football in China.

Football cartoon - Chinese style.

Famous Players:

Household football names in China mean nothing to outsiders, except perhaps for the keenest football follower - who has a special interest towards the sport in Asia. But there are at least a few deserving of special mention, who mean much to the Chinese fans.

Rong Zhihang, is regarded as the most accomplished player in Chinese football history. He was born in 1948, on the 30th July (ironically just one day later and his birthday would coincide with one of the Country's leading Clubs - Ba Yi or '1st August'!). He was a strong attacking half-back (midfielder in today's terminology), and with his excellent ball skills became known as 'The Pele of China'. Born in the Guangdong (Canton) Province, he had trials for the Guangzhou Workers team, and despite his lack of physical development at that time (he was only 16 years old), his ball skills were noted, and he was retained by the Club. However, the political situation denied him any competitive matches, until 1971, when he was brought on as a substitute in a Guangzhou Friendly match against Cuba. The visitors, although only 1-0 ahead were playing by far the better football, but Rong's appearance changed the match, and after creating the equaliser, he became a local hero overnight with his dribbling in the opposition penalty area, before scoring the local team's match winner. Rong's skilful play was soon noted further afield, and as China played an ever-increasing number of games, by 1977 until 1980, he was a virtual ever-present in the National team. After the new York Cosmos match against China in 1978, the visiting star Pele remarked of Rong: " *His ball control, shooting and playmaking ability have made me feel sorry for having presumed that China had yet to produce a superstar*". His abilities were recognised by his nomination as one of China's top ten sportsmen for three consecutive years - an unheard of feat for a footballer.

Although he decided to retire in 1980, he was persuaded to make a comeback the following year, and proved his worth, helping the team to win their preliminary World Cup group - which included a victory over North Korea (the first for 20 years). In a final qualifying match against New Zealand he was badly fouled and had to be carried off, missing the return leg which was lost to the Kiwis. Although not fully fit, he returned for the other four Cup games, in which he set-up most of the goals (and scored one). China came their closest ever to the World Cup Finals, but New Zealand (after a play-off game) won the ticket to Spain, and so Rong was denied his chance on the World stage. He finally retired soon after.

Gu Guangming was another player who came from Southern China, and was born on the 31st of January 1959. As a member of the Guangdong Province team, he won many honours, and was one of the leading players in the National squad around the early 1980's period. He was a fast winger with a good shot (scoring four goals in the 1982 World Cup preliminary games). He particularly impressed in the National team's matches in 1984, and Hamburger SV of West Germany were keen to sign him. This would have made Gu the first Chinese football 'export', but the political climate at that time denied him the opportunity. The following year he was voted the '1984 Asian Footballer Of The Year' runner-up.

Gu Guangming

Post-War Champions:

Note: The definition of 'Champions' is difficult to fully appreciate, since over the past 50 or so years the methods of determination have varied. The early post-war years saw the football played principally in Shanghai, which has determined, on the next page, the 'League Champions' for that period. In 1951 there was a national competition, and the following year there was no competition.

1953 saw a re-organisation whereby the four most prominent teams played-off in Shanghai. Later, between 1966 and 1972 there was no officially recognised competitive football, and when the irregular National Athletics meeting have been staged, the football Championship has been suspended that year, the Champions being determined by a football tournament in one centre competed for by a number of selected Clubs. 1984 saw the Championship decided by a three week knock-out tournament in Wuhan.

Travel within such a vast country is obviously a great problem, but it appears that football is now being played at the top level on a truly national basis. It is also relevant to note that the 1994 League is now sponsored, being known as the 'Marlboro League'. Divisions have been noted numerically (e.g. 'First') for convenience, but over the years the prefix has varied (currently the 'First' Division is known as 'Group A'). A short report of early fixtures for the 1994 season, in the *China Daily* (English language) newspaper, stated: " *Twelve teams ..... are competing in China's first ever formal league play*" (the meaning of which, I have to confess, I do not understand!)

The team (town and province) spellings are given in 'pinyin' (as opposed to traditional), the 'phonetic transcription' of the Chinese words, which became the official romanised spelling in 1958, and is now generally used throughout the world.

Other prominent players who did make the move to the West include, **Zuo Shusheng** - the Chinese National team Captain - who went to Holland, **Liu Haiguang** who played in Yugoslavia and **Jia Xiuquan** who also went to this now tragically split Country, where he was nicknamed "Jia-wa". The mid-1980's had seen the rise of Jia Xiuquan - who hailed from Dalian - to prominence, for three years (from 1984) he was arguably the most popular player in China, a centre-half he was an 'export' to Partisan Belgrade. Leading striker Liu Haiquang was the leading scorer in 1987, with 30 goals to his credit.

Lee Feng Lu was born in 1911, and was a pre-war prominent member of the North China squad, who played for the Pei Hwa and later Pei Ning teams. He was a graduate of Fu Jen University, Peking. After the Second World War he was appointed as coach to both the People's Liberation Army and the National teams, and after a period from 1956 as Vice-President, he went on to become the President of the Chinese Football Association.

League Champions:

1946	Tsing Peh	1973	Beijing
1947	Tung Hwa	1974	Ba Yi
1948	Tung Hwa/Tsing Peh (joint)	1975	Guangxi
1949	Tsing Peh	1976	Beijing
1950	No Competition	1977	Ba Yi
1951	North-East (Bei Tung)	1978	Liaoning
1952	No Competition	1979	Guangtung
1953	Ba Yi	1980	Tianjin
1954	North-East	1981	Ba Yi
1955	Central Inst.of Physical Culture(Beijing)	1982	Beijing
1956	No Competition	1983	Shanghai
1957	Tianjin	1984	Beijing
1958	Beijing	1985	Liaoning
1959	Ba Yi	1986	Ba Yi
1960	Tianjin	1987	Guangdong
1961	Shanghai	1988	Liaoning
1962	Shanghai	1989	Liaoning
1963	Beijing Youth	1990	Liaoning
1964	Beijing Physical Culture Inst.	1991	Liaoning
1965	Jilin	1992	Liaoning (believed)
1966 - 1972	No Competition	1993	Liaoning (believed)

There are no doubt other competitions, both National and Regional but details do not appear to be available. An 'F.A.Cup' type competition was introduced where selected Clubs (1st Division, several 2nd and the 3rd Champions) congregate in a prominent City, and games are played on a knock-out basis, but this was to determine the overall Champions of the country. The first such tournament was held in October 1984 in Wuhan, a City near Shanghai, on the River Yangtse. I was told by one fan, that this system was not popular, and the spectators would prefer a European style F.A.Competition.

Composition of Leagues (1994):

There is a National First Division, plus a Second Division (also believed National), and several regionalised Third Divisions. At one time the Third Division (one or more) was effectively composed of Youth teams. I was informed (correctly?) that such teams are now separate Clubs.

- 1994 Season -

1st Division	2nd Division
Ba Yi ('1st August')	Foshan
Beijing	Guangxi *
Dalian	Guangzhou 2nd Team
Guangdong *	Houo-Che-Tou
Guangzhou	Hubei *
Jiangsu	Hunan *
Jilin *	Qingdao
Liaoning *	Tianjin
Shangdong *	Tianjin (2nd Team)
Shanghai	Wuhan
Shenyang	Kunming (?)
Sichuan *	Shaanxi * (?)

* Indicates a Province Club

The Clubs:

A 'Club' can take several different formats, and for one period even the National 'B' team was in the First Division. Currently the First and Second Divisions, consist of 'City' teams, Province teams (noted * previously), Second teams (believed unusual in China for such 'Reserve' XI's in a competitive form) and Representative teams. Ba Yi (translated 'August 1st') - is the National Army team and Houo-Che-Tou, the Railway Club; both based in Beijing.

The 'Guiness Book of World Soccer' (pub.1992) states that Wuhan is represented by Hebei Football Club which I believe is incorrect (2 different Clubs), and Nanjing plus Kunming are also stated as being the Nanjing and Kunming Army Unit teams which cannot be confirmed (although it is believed that the Jiangsu team is based in Nanjing, and may once have been the Army team under that City's name).

At one time many of the 'Clubs' were Army teams of the Province or City, but it appears that this aspect has been in most cases dropped from their titles. With the changing political situation throughout the world in the last twenty years or so, there has been less threat from others, and therefore it is possible that in China their military might, in respect of sport, has been less emphasised. It should be noted that the Province teams (currently 7 of the 12 team First Division) do not have a fixed 'home' ground as such, but play such games in different towns within the Province. The most popular venue is likely to be in the capital of the Province, and some Cities in fact have two Stadiums - one for the 'town' Club, and one for the Provincial team.

As a comparison the membership of the 16 strong First Division ten years ago differed as follows:
1984 included Tianjing (1st and 2nd teams) - now both in the Second Division. Beijing Army Unit (now the 'Ba Yi' club) Shenyang Army Unit (Same as 1994 Shenyang?). Nanjing Army Unit (believed may now be Jiangsu team). Kunming Army Unit (may now be 2nd Division). Hebei and Hubei (both now 2nd Division), and Anhui (no longer in either Division).

The 'newcomers' by 1994, were: Dalian, Jilin (who in fact were withdrawn during the 1984 season), Guangzhou, and Jiangshu.

Ba Yi (or '1st August'). This Club is the most symbolic in the Chinese League, for its name refers to the founding date of the National Army which its team represents. The team was previously known as 'The People's Liberation Army'. The team is based in Beijing, and Shirt colours are believed to be yellow. Ba Yi are one of the most prominent of Chinese teams, with five title successes (the last coming in 1986), and their success is no doubt due to the vast number of - potentially - the best athletic players.

Beijing. Being the capital city, with a population approaching 10 million (covering an area nearly 17,000 sq.km.) they are also one of the top sides as would be expected. They too have won the League Championship on five occasions - their success last in 1984.

Dalian. Along with Shanghai, Dalian is an area with a football history that goes back one of the longest. Dalian is situated on the southern tip of Liaodong peninsular, in North-east China's Liaoning province. Although the provincial Dalian team have never won a Championship (fourth has been the best placing), it was one of the pre-war treaty ports, and so has known football for around a century. The Loghua team of 1929 consisted of players principally from Dalian, who thrashed the touring Japanese champions team by 7-0. The first (communist) Championship won in 1951 by the North-East China team was also composed mainly of Dalian players, and for many years the City have supplied more than their fair share of National squad members, including Jia Xiuquan a 'star' of the 1980's. Football is the most popular sport in the City, especially amongst the Shipyard workers.

Guangdong. This provincial (Canton) team won the Championship once, in 1987, but is known for its nurturing of many successful players, the most famous of all being Rong Zhihang, also Gu Guangming. The Province is the most progressive (and richest), and therefore has probably exploited commercialism in football far more than elsewhere. They, together with Shanghai play the 'South China Tiger' style of football, relying on skill and fast short passing. The team play (or at least used to) in dowdy beige coloured shirts.

Guangzhou. The 'Gateway' to China - to or from the South (Hong Kong) - where most tourists pass through. The City has two major Stadiums, one for the City team and the other used by the Province. The City has known football for many years, often staging important representative matches. They have yet to win their first Championship. Like the Provincial team their shirt colours used to be a somewhat discreet colour (browny/orange).

Jiangsu. This Province team (I believe) is based in the former capital, Nanjing, about 200

Dalian Shipyard - where football is the most popular sport.

kilometres East of Shanghai, where there is the large Wutaishan Stadium. They have yet to win a Championship, and do not appear to feature prominently in Chinese football.

Jilin. Champions just once, in 1965, the yellow-shirted Jilin team is another Province side. Changchun is the capital of this 1.5 million populated City, the 'motortown' of China and also renowned for its Film Studios - but not apparently the football team!

Liaoning. Without doubt the Country's leading team with their incredible current run of Championship victories. Prior to this sequence they were also the winners in 1978 and 1985, the latter year saw their 'B' team as Second Division Champions. The Province of Liaoning lies North-east of Beijing, South-west of Jilin Province, with its main town being Shenyang. The population of this principal town, and in the former Country of Manchuria, shot up from 100,000 in 1910, to its current 5.5 million. In addition the Province has the slightly smaller town of Dalian (4.6 million). Therefore with 25% of the First Division in this fairly small Province (Liaoning, Dalian and Shenyang), it can really be compared - on a much larger geographical scale - as the footballing North-east of China, to the North-east of England.

Shangdong. This Province is on the coast, between Shanghai and Beijing, and the team appear to be nothing more than a 'run of the mill' team. The principal city is Jinan - an industrialised and somewhat polluted area. Matches played here are at the Shangdong Provincial Stadium (between Qianfoshan and Wenhua Dong Roads) in the southern area of the city. The Club colours are yellow.

Shanghai. Of all the pre-war Chinese cities, Shanghai was the most westernised, being the most important of the treaty ports. The modern version of football in China was developed in the City (by foreigners), and Shanghai was one of the first to attract the locals to the sport. It is a vast City, the fifth largest in the World, with a population of over 12 million, and although now very much an area of decaying splendour, it is the most westernised - albeit in an old-fashioned way - City in China. The legacy of pre-war football coupled with its large population has made the football team - which play in blue shirts - one of the leaders, although they have only won the Championship once in recent years (1983). The Stadium, in the North-east of the city is covered in detail elsewhere.

Shenyang. The capital of the football stronghold province of Liaoning, with a population of 5.5 million, yet despite the successes of the Province team - which no doubt play some of their matches in the City - it is very much a poor relation, having no Championships to its credit. The club colours are red, and the previous Shenyang Army Unit team may be one and the same with the current Club.

Sichuan. Despite being the most populated Province in China, the representative team has never won a Championship. The Province is a large one, situated to the South-west of the Country, adjacent to Tibet. The capital, Chengdu is an agricultural centre, with the People's Stadium, located in the centre of the City, although apparently the smaller City of Chonquing (to the North) is the hotbed of football in this region. The club colours are believed to be green.

A brief look at the Second Division (Unfortunately I have been unable to identify with certainty all 12 current member-teams):
There are three (or four) Province teams, **Guanxi, Hunan** and **Hubei,** which are located by coincidence adjacent to each other (South to North), in the South-east of the Country. **Shaanxi** is also a possible team in this Division. I have seen several references to this Provincial team, and as I visited the People's Stadium there, in Xi'an, I would like to think it was one! Surprisingly both the first and second teams of **Tianjin** (the third largest City in China, a two-hour train ride East of Beijing), are in the Division, together with **Guangzhou 'Reserves',** the only other 'B' team. **Foshan,** principally a folk-craft centre, on Chinese standards is a small City (population c.200,000), lying just to the South-west of Guangzhou, and was the first sponsored Club in the country.

Qingdao, another City in the 'football-mad' Shangdong Province, was a lesser known treaty port (principally German), whilst **Wuhan,** is the Capital of the Hubei province, and is the collective name given to the three municipalities of Wuchang, Hankou, and Hanyang. **Kunming,** is the capital of the most South-western Province of Yunnan, with the Tuodong Stadium in the middle of town. **Houo-che-tou,** is a railway team (once an important feature of pre-war football) based in Beijing.

A very brief visit to just a Club's Stadium can hardly provide a detailed history, but it does give a 'feel' for the subject, and also allows comparisons between the venues. In my relatively brief (and at times frustratingly difficult) adventures, I managed to find and see something of each of the following: First Division: The two main Stadiums in Beijing (possibly where both First Division teams play), Shanghai, Guangdong, Guangzhou, and Jiangsu (i.e. six of the twelve).

Second Division: Guanxi (Guilin), Guangzhou reserves, plus possibly Houo-che-tou (Beijing), and Shaanxi i.e. up to 4 of the 12.
Others: Wuxi and Suzhou (which may also host provincial First Division matches) in the Jiangsu province. Also the most basic 'Ground' near Guilin, i.e. 3 'non-League' venues!

The layout of the Hong Kou Stadium - the home of First Division Shanghai.

Clubs of the past:

The pre-war Clubs (particularly those of the foreigners) have been mentioned briefly in the 'History' section. **Shanghai F.C.** was the first (in 1888) followed by **Shanghai Recreation Club** the same year. In 1902, the original 'Shanghai' appears to have disappeared, and the recreation Club adopted the name. The post-war football situation in the Country is of course totally alien to earlier times (more so even than Hong Kong), where it is reasonable to conclude that none of the present Clubs have any relationship with those of the past. **Tung Hwa**, probably the most successful of the pre-war Chinese Clubs, were one of the few that survived briefly during the early post-war years. The team won the Championship in two of the four pre-reformation years of 1946 to 1949. The Club was founded in 1930, and soon rose to prominence, aided in no small way by the defection of several top players from other Shanghai Clubs. The team withdrew from the League in 1949, and with the communists taking over later that year, the Club disappeared completely. **Tsing Peh,** had a very short, but very successful existence. They were formed in 1946 from an amalgamation of the pre-war San Hsing and Lien Nee Clubs, plus several unattached players. The team won the Shanghai League in 1946 and 1949, and were joint-holders in 1948, but they too of course disappeared soon after their last Championship victory. In Peking (Beijing), the railway team **Pei Ning** was the leading team in the 1920's and 30's, and frequent North China Champions. During this period, **Police** were the leaders in Canton (Guangzhou), **Chung Hua** led the way in the treaty port of Tientsin (Tianjin), and **King Hua** were the best in the capital Nanking (Nanjing).

Lido were formed in September 1938 (by entrepreneur W.T.Kao), and denied immediate entry into the Shanghai First Division, with their top stars they won all eight Third Division games (including a 26-1 mauling of Sokol), plus the Skottowe Cup. The earlier years saw **Three Cultures** become the first Chinese Club to be admitted to the Shanghai League - in 1926 - and that same year **Loh Hwa** were the Champions, in their formation year, of the Chinese League in Shanghai. The latter team was created by Yui En Tse, a well known sportsman and entrepreneur (the team played in black and white stripes in admiration of their mentors - Newcastle United). Internal strife split the Club in 1930, and it soon faded away. Aside from Shanghai, **Ching Hua** was one of the earliest of Chinese Clubs, founded in 1909, they came from Mei Hsien in the Kwantung (Canton and later Guangdong) Province. In the pre-war days, and within the treaty enclaves themselves, there were of course numerous teams composed of foreigners that fought out their League and Cup matches, **Shanghai F.C., Navy, Police, Deluge Co., Recreation, College, St.John's, Union, Artillery, Engineers,** to name but a few. Additionally 'International' teams were formed in Shanghai - composed of players from those countries, notably England and later Portugal. By the late 1940's these teams were no more, no longer were the treaty ports as such functioning, and by then the game had been given over - or more realistically taken over - by the Chinese, who were by then part of the new regime. One final point on the subject, what became of **Wan Chengde,** the first privately sponsored Club in the country?

International Football:

In the post-war years such top level football was limited to touring teams (both into and out of China), although these were very often individual Clubs representing their Country. Notably two such tours were made by 'China', to Australia, in the 1920's. The first named 'China' match was against the Philippines in Manila during February 1913, a 2-1 defeat for the foreigners, for what is considered the first ever International match in Asia.

Two years later, in Shanghai, China beat the same opponents. The tournament, known as the Far-Eastern Games, was held normally every other year, until 1934, with Japan later entering the competition, and China always triumphed - except for the last series, when they shared the honour with Japan. It could be said that true International matches did not start until the post-war years, and China's self-isolation, plus their attitude to certain Countries, particularly Taiwan, has resulted in their general non-participation in Asian and World competitions until fairly recent years. Currently there are numerous competitions held in Asia, and these coupled with Friendly matches (the Chinese always used to regard their foreign sorties with an emphasis on 'friendly') has led to vast numbers of such encounters.

In the major tournaments, the Chinese have performed badly, although their recent attitude and determination, coupled with their vast manpower on which to call upon, suggests that this situation could well change before too long. China's first foray into the World Cup did not come until 1978, but their results have generally been poor, and the closest to qualification for the final rounds (in 1986) has already been related. Entry was made for the Olympic Games in 1936 and again twelve years later. After missing out in 1952, they qualified in 1956 - only to withdraw later. It was 1986 before their next appearance, from which time they have been involved on each occasion. But only in 1988 did they achieve any success, after successfully negotiating the qualifying hurdle, but they lost in the finals, in the first round. The Asian Championship has seen China have more success, although the competition was not entered until 1976. After failure with their first two attempts, they reached the overall Finals in 1984 and in 1988. Likewise the Asian Games saw the absence of the Chinese until 1978 - when they fought through to the semi-finals,

and were losing quarter-finalists on the next three accessions (including 1990 when China were the hosts) in this four- yearly tournament.

In the Asian Champion Teams Cup, a team was not entered until 1985 - Liaoning - and the only real achievement has been that same Club's run through to the end, which they lost in the two-legged final to Nisson of Japan. A mystery year was 1988, when China's representative was a Club by the name of Wan Bao (which presumably is/was a corporation Club, perhaps a Railways or Steelworks team, etc.), but apart from not hearing of this Club elsewhere, Guangdong were the previous years Chinese Champions! In the Asian Cup-Winners Cup (started in 1990), no Chinese team has reached the semi-final stage. The only real success story has been in the Asian Youth Cup, which saw China as the winners in 1984.

Lesser competitions have produced a few victories - the Merdeka Tournament (which includes a number of foreign representative teams) was first entered in 1984, and seven years later the Chinese reached the final; they won the Piala Kemerdekaan Independence Cup (not exactly a World famous competition!) in 1988, plus the President's Gold Cup (in Bangladesh) - 1982 - the Merlion Cup (held in Singapore), in 1986, and the Indonesian 'Marah Halin Cup' five years later. Success on the World stage has certainly eluded China to date.

Bits and Pieces:

There was no pre-war National Football League. The coastal treaty ports and Peking, had strongly contested local Leagues.

Match attendances: Only a few sketchy figures have been traced for post-war matches. A popular Club (e.g. Shanghai) can attract around 10,000 on average, which can rise to 30,000 for a top clash. Crowds at International matches, or those against visiting touring sides can increase to 80,000 in the Workers Stadium Beijing. The popularity of football in China is often stated, and whilst these figures appear to be quite impressive, it has to be considered that in, say Shanghai, with a population of some 12 million (far more than London), there is just **one** Senior club, and probably few others.

Football is popular amongst those who choose to support it, but overall it does not have great appeal (supposedly the fourth or fifth most popular sport).

The most popular areas for Football in China are in the North-east (in the relatively small Liaoning Province) and the far South - the Guangdong (Canton) Province. I was told that in general football is becoming increasingly popular throughout the Country, especially at Universities (completing the 'circle' for this was one of the birthplaces of the pre-war game amongst the locals).

TV is now widely seen in China, and much football is featured from Europe.

The Chinese Football season lasts from April to November, and countrywide the temperatures must vary considerably (equally as they would should the season extend over the European Winter period). Matches are normally played on a Sunday, and very occasionally midweek.... Programmes, I believe, are unheard of in China - although I would think it likely that 'brochure type' publications are produced for tournament matches. There are one (or more) Soccer Newspaper, published weekly or possibly more often.... Admission prices: I was told 2 to 3 yuan (around 12 to 20p) is normall with this price doubling for big matches. Wages: There is now an open market for players, and a top player can expect about 30,000 yuan per year (around £2,000), which is comparitively a very high salary.

The popularity and success in the Liaoning Province, I was told, was due to the people being generally taller - and therefore physically more dominant - in this area than elsewhere.

The China National Amateur Athletic Federation (which included the Chinese F.A.) was founded in Nanking (Nanjing) in 1924. This organisation governed football played by the locals. Earlier in 1910, the Shanghai F.A. was formally recognised, but this was predominantly foreigner based.

Naturally China is pinning its hopes on the youth, and in April 1994 it was announced that the Yunnan Yu'an Iron and Steel Co. Ltd. donated one million yuan (about £60,000) to the national Youth team, and will continue to donate the same amount each year until 1998. I believe that at the season's end there is a play-off amongst the Champions of the third Divisions (two?), to decide the one promotion to Division 1.

Many First Division teams are now sponsored, and the Sponsor's name is unofficially attached to the Club name. Most Clubs have a squad of around 24 players, and in general they do not have formal (competitive) Reserve teams.

> THREE strong northeastern teams all lost in the second-round of the '94 Marlboro League China national division one Group A competition on Sunday. Sichuan overwhelmed Jilin 4-0, Shenyang and Shandong nipped Dalian and Liaoning with an identical score of 1-0. Shanghai chalked up their second win in as many matches when they edged Beijing 4-3. The army beat Guangdong 1-0 and Jiangsu, following their first-round 1-1 tie with the army, were held to draw again by Guangzhou, 0-0. Besides Shanghai, Shandong and Sichuan had also scored two wins. Twelve teams, considered China's best, are competing in China's first-ever formal league play.
> (Agencies — CD)

> CHINA'S determination to raise its soccer standard got a major boost on Tuesday when Yunnan Yu'an Iron and Steel Co Ltd donated one million yuan to the Chinese national youth team. Totally out of their love for China's soccer, the company will also donate one million yuan each year till 1998.
> (Xinhua — Agencies — CD)

Newspapers: pre-war there were several English language newspapers, and football information was often carried in great detail. *The China Daily* is now the only such newspaper, and information on the sport is somewhat sketchy; the two articles above were included in the sports news during April 1994.

Fat Kwong Street to Guangdong - and onwards.
A Personal Experience

Travellers to China and Hong Kong more often carry out their journey in that order. We didn't, we did it in reverse. From Hong Kong to Guangdong (Canton) and upwards on the map to Beijing. One is suddenly thrown into an alien environment, where car horns and bicycle bells assault the ears, and those same vehicles (until you get the hang of crossing a road which is alive with slow moving wall-to-wall traffic) could assault your body.

The Guangdong Province of China, or more particularly Guangzhou, must be the most traffic congested town on Earth (or so we thought until we experienced most of the other towns on our route, which also vie for this dubious honour). You quickly have to learn a few road rules.

1. The most dangerous place to cross the road is at a black and white striped area that looks confusingly like a pedestrian crossing. They probably were intended as such, but there the similarity ends. Dangerous, because you have an inherent feeling that they **should** be safe, but in reality they are completely disregarded by the near 24 hour rush-hour traffic on its scurrying way to who knows where.
2. You do not wait for the road, or even one lane to clear. If you do then it would be advisable to have provisions with you for your long wait. The answer is to move step by step across the road, as each step width is clear - the bikes and motor vehicles won't run you over - providing you take things calmly - you will be assailed with the blaring of horns and the tinkling of bells - not out of impatience but simply to warn you not be too adventurous. It takes nerve, but with a strong will and courage, you will reach your goal - the far side of the road.
3. Do not assume that the pavements are solely for pedestrians. Should you unwisely assume this, then you will soon be shaken out of your reverie, by yet more bicycle bells, whose operators - frustrated by the congestion on the road - will also takeover the footpaths.

This is of course somewhat irrelevant with regard to football you may say, but it does provide an insight into one of the difficulties of reaching a Ground on foot.

Canton - can do:

A Groundhopper could hardly ask for more in China. Not one, but two First Division Grounds, and possibly a third Stadium also used for football if you have time in Guangdong. Each is fairly easily accessible, aided by an excellent, readily available tourist street map. Arriving late afternoon there was little that could be done footballwise, other than to study the map for the following day's itinerary - for one day was all that was available to me. After doing the tourist 'bit' during the first part of the morning, I couldn't believe my luck when our bus turned off Jiefang Road North, and into Yuexiu Park. This park was created in the 1950's as a large recreation area, from a former desolate hilly area named Guangyin Hill. After the bus pulls into the car park the standard tourist hike is to climb the hill and see the impressive statue of the five goats, which commemorates Guangzhou's mythical origins. But who could resist instead, just a few hundred metres along the path, the Yuexiushan People's Stadium - presumably the home Ground of Guangzhou F.C. The Chinese tour guide thought I should have resisted this delight, however I went all the same (incidentally this was the only standard tourist attraction on our itinerary that I had to forego).

The Ground is in a peculiar - if picturesque - location. High up on the hill, overlooked by tall trees, yet apparently open to free viewing on a matchday. Perhaps they close the park, except for paying football spectators. Unfortunately I only had my camcorder (My wife - who went to see the goats - had one still camera, and the 'reserve' was in the hotel), which is fine for viewing in the armchair later, but not ideal for producing illustrations in this book! Fortunately this was the only occasion during my excursions when I was without a 'still' camera.

The Stadium consists of a vast oval amphitheatre, not unlike an unroofed Wembley Stadium (and not much smaller), with a capacity for at least 50,000 I would think. All seated - high concrete steps in rings all round - four large floodlight pylons, but with little cover. At one end there is a cantilevered roof, about 70 metres long, and along one side a boxed-in and roofed Stand of similar length.

Yuexiushan People's Stadium

Still photo's taken from my camcorder shots, and consequently somewhat poor. Note the elaborate entrance (top), and (bottom), the general lack of cover but high terracing.

The most striking feature is at the other end of the Stadium, where the main entrance consists of three high triumphal arches, flanked by brick towers and roofed - looking not unlike a gigantic Chinese teahouse. I had little time to explore (one lesson that must be adhered to on these diversions is never arrive back late to the coach - your fellow passengers and guides will accept your madness, but not tolerate your bad manners), but I was able to walk around the upper rim at one end and one side. The path I took dropped down towards the 'triumphal arches', and given time I could probably have found my way to the stadium ground level and explore inside. But I had to make do with this somewhat cursory view, and then quickly scurry back to my fellow passengers. Retracing my route, I still couldn't see how they could attract paying customers here, for the high level view was only obscured by a thin chain link fence.

The walk - up a steep hill along the flat - down a steep hill - and then the reverse, was quite exhausting, but thankfully there was a soft drink stall where I could quench my thirst. Yes it was 'coke', and yes in the town there are 'MacDonalds' and 'Kentucky Fried Chicken' establishments too!

Our return to the Hotel (the most impressive 'Garden Hotel' - we were to have stayed in the renowned 'White Swan', but a bigwig meeting of party officials had taken late notice preference) in mid-afternoon, was ideal for another exploration. The Garden Hotel is situated about 1 kilometre North of the Guangdong People's Stadium, just off Zhongshan Road 3. This was my first solo experience at crossing roads, nearly being run down on pavements, and getting stuck in pedestrian traffic jams on footbridges! The Stadium here is very big and very neat, but incongruously jammed between narrow and busy streets of little shops.

I managed to find an open entrance, and found inside several training sessions going on for various sports. The football coaching was the major activity, with two separate groups, one for under 12's or so, and the other for those up to about 16 years old. This was the only occasion in China where I saw formal coaching of youngsters taking place, and amongst the older group their was one boy who showed exceptional ball control skill, and was only too pleased to show off in front of the camcorder. Unusually for China, this was a well covered Stadium, and I would think reasonably modern. The photographs tell most of the story, and on this occasion I actually had time to sit down, have a good look, and also make a close estimate of the capacity. With 25 tiers of seats, and 6 sections distinctly separated by different colours, the Ground would hold about 35,000, all seated; the seats had no backs, but were individual, rather than a continuous bench arrangement.

The temptation was to explore further, for according to the map there were two more Stadiums nearby, but as they appeared on the map to be very basic (no apparent raised terracing), I made my weary - and intrepid route back to the Hotel. There was another possible Ground that is used for football, that at the Tian He Sports Centre, on the Eastern outskirts, along Huan Shi Dong Lu (Road), but about 5 kilometres from the Hotel. There was no time for this one, and therefore its details will have to remain a mystery.

I was subsequently told that there is another Club in Guangzhou, that of Apollo, which has taken the name of its sponsor, a Chemical Company, but I was unable to determine this Club's status.

Guangzhou had been a very rewarding football start to China (despite finding it impossible to find any English speaker who had any idea about football in the Country). Two Stadiums easily found, with time to spare, and an excellent map - I had been spoilt, for the other Cities were going to prove much more difficult.

Formal training session in Guangdong Stadium.

An impressive view from the top of the Stands in the Guangdong People's Stadium....

.... But, a far from impressive approach to the main entrance of the Stadium.

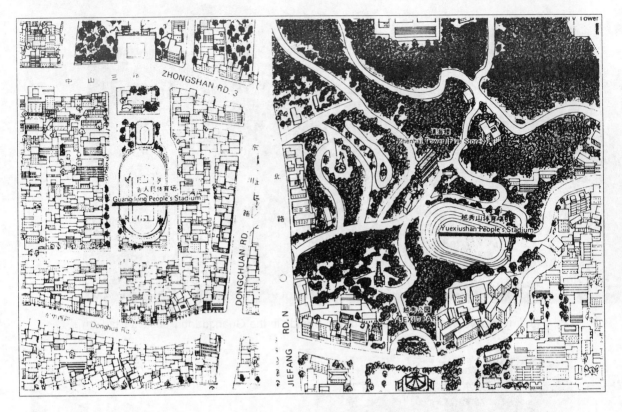

The two Stadiums. (Left) Guangdong in a built-up area, and (right) Yeuxishan in a park.

Gorging in Guilin

The main Stadium in Guilin (opposite the main entrance side). The only raised viewing areas
- the open Stand (complete with flats and washing on top!), and a few steps adjacent.

Guilin, is the personification of China - open countryside, vast boggy paddy field with farmers in Coolie hats urging on their docile water buffalo. Footballwise, there was little to see. The 'Stadium' (and I use the word in its loosest sense) was obviously also used for football since there were goalposts at each end - possibly originals from the pre-communist era! The grass was roughly cut (and I mean rough), a fairly even surface, but not a trace of pitch markings for football or any other sport. There was no raised terracing, except for an incongruous, fairly high, two tier open seated Stand, about 25 metres long and tucked in one corner. The most amazing sight was the upper portion which appeared to have been let as flats, with several families and their washing on view! It looked as if the intention was to continue this Stand all round the pitch - starting and finishing in this corner - but possibly funds soon ran out, and apart from a few steps of open terrace adjacent, this constituted the spectator facilities. The main entrance was off Central Zhongshan Road in the centre of town, and probably the major sporting facility here was the large Hall which ran alongside this side of the pitch.

During an evening stroll we were 'adopted' by a young man who spoke good English, and although he knew little about football, I managed to glean some information, which hopefully is correct.

Guilin is not a 'football town' (that I can believe), although there are several teams in the town, the major one only aspires to a Provincial League status, playing before crowds of a few hundred - on a good day! According to one map that I saw, there was another Stadium on the Southern outskirts of town, hidden behind the large apartment buildings off Shanghai Road. Yet despite two journeys which passed the site on the tourist bus, my eagle eye could see nothing - not even a rusty goalpost.

The highlight of Guilin is the gorges, by the trip down the Li River, a beautiful journey through the weird round topped hills unique to this region. The trip starts at Zhujian, a small town 22 km. from Guilin, and low and behold a football ground, of a sort. It was unfenced and unterraced, but it did have reasonable cut grass, plus a marked pitch and goalposts - definitely a 'Guilin & District League Division 1' venue I would think! None the less, it was the only football pitch, as opposed to Stadium, that I saw in China.

Guilin isn't a groundhoppers dream, but it is a very pleasant area, free of the hustle seen elsewhere. With a population of some 300,000 including a large percentage of minorities. And where else can you see ballroom dancing by the locals on the promenade beside the Li River outside your Hotel at 6.30 a.m.?

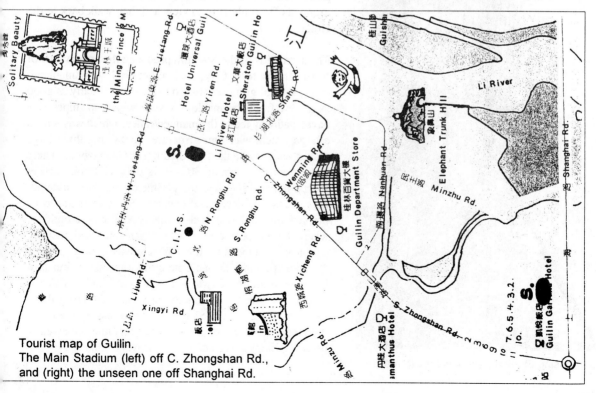

Tourist map of Guilin.
The Main Stadium (left) off C. Zhongshan Rd.,
and (right) the unseen one off Shanghai Rd.

On to the Warriors

A depressing Stadium, and weather to match!

Xi'an became a tourist area after the discovery of the terracotta army not far away, but the City was supposedly at one time the largest City in the World, and currently with a near 3 million population it is no small town. It is the capital of the Shaanxi Province, and therefore is a base for a relatively senior team (possibly of the Second Division). There appeared to be three Stadiums in Xi'an, one within the walled City - the Xi'an People's Stadium - which I was unable to get anywhere near (it was miles from the Hotel), the Provincial Stadium (just outside the walls) which is an indoor arena, and the Shaanxi People's Stadium, conveniently located about 2 km. from the Orient Hotel where we stayed. Despite its closeness, it was here that I encountered my first (of several) ground-hopping problems. With drizzle falling I left the Hotel at 7.00 a.m., assured by reception that the best Stadium was just a 20 minute walk (at a brisk pace it took thirty) along the Xiao Zhai Road. According to my map the location was the Shaanxi History Museum. But undeterred, with umbrella held high I navigated the uneven pavement, and crossed several wide roads at my peril, that were packed with traffic. I reached my goal to find that it was the site of - the Shaanxi History Museum! I should have headed North from the Hotel instead, a shorter distance, as my map and my intuition had told me. But luck was on my side for on our return from the Terracotta Army, we passed the Ground, off Zhu Que Street, and I asked to be dropped off - preferring to view and then walk back to the Hotel.

The surrounds of the Stadium produced the appearance of fortifications to a City, and although I was unable to enter, several glimpses from outside was virtually as good as a view from the inside. A very wide and impressive paved pathway led to the main entrance, which was within a large watchtower type structure, containing three large arches - not unlike the first Stadium at Guangzhou. There were frequent - about 30 - exit only (I think) arches spaced regularly around the perimeter, but the surroundings shouted of decay and neglect. Some exits had been bricked up, and one had a shanty building around it, where there appeared to be an independent small business operating! Opposite the 'Watchtower', was another entrance, possibly at one time quite impressive, but now left to deteriorate. It was still wet, and I had to risk life and limb climbing up muddy rises and slithering down slippery slopes. Tucked in the part-recesses created by the piers of the perimeter wall, the Stadium appeared to be the unlikely local version of 'Lovers Lane'.

Difficult when you had to stand near them to take photo's - of the Stadium. It is a large Stadium, with floodlights but no cover, continuous concrete bench seating, and a capacity for about 30,000. The weather contributed to my leaving this Ground slightly depressed.

It was big enough for large crowds, but somehow I think they must have occurred some years ago. At least the walk back to the Hotel was exciting. It's bad enough having to cross a road in China, but on this walk at one point the pavement had just disappeared (they were building an underpass there), and pedestrians had to join the dense traffic in the road.

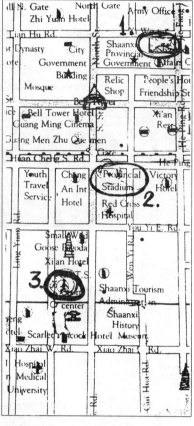

(Above) Xi'an main streets plan.
1. Xi'an People's Stadium.
2. Provincial (indoor) Stadium.
3. Shaanxi Provincial People's Stadium (that was visited).

(Top) The three-arched main entrance, (left) one of the many exits set in the fortrees-like walls.

Hong Kou Stadium - Shanghai
(Top) Behind one goal (with monument and video screen), (below) The main Stand

(Above) Behind the other goal (the sports hall - top right).

(Left) The austere main entrance (elephant sculpture in the extreme bottom left corner).

(Below) Shanghai road map (Northeast of City), the former football venue (Jiangwan Stadium), and the current one (Hong Kou), which was visited.

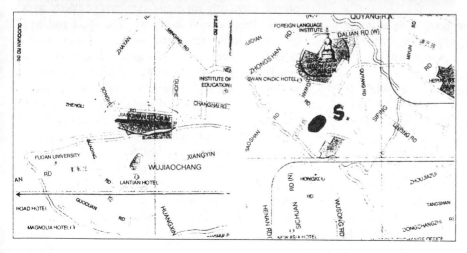

Intrigue in Shanghai.

I looked forward to the visit to Shanghai. For in a sense this was where, in Chinese football terms, it really all started. With much of the famous old Bund still standing alongside the waterfront, Shanghai has retained much of its pre-war intrigue and mystery..... the days of gangsters, spies and illicit dealing. It also has a very good Stadium.

By pure luck a chance meeting with Deng Jun Feng who worked at the Jianguo Hotel where we stayed for two nights provided me with a wealth of information about the local scene. I was becoming somewhat frustrated, for the few English speakers that I spoke to obviously had no knowledge of football in China. Unfortunately the apparent attitude in China is that in order to avoid causing offence, or their loss of face, they will never deny knowing anything, therefore much of what you are informed may well be incorrect! Deng's English was reasonably good, but more important he was a keen fan, his team being the local Shanghai club. In fact he offered to take me to a top match the following Sunday, when the locals were playing Beijing. Typically by the following Sunday we were due to be well on our way - to Beijing. I was able to quiz him for about an hour, and many of the modern facts previously stated came from this conversation. Now how to get to Hong Kou Stadium ? To put things into perspective, the population of Shanghai and its environs is over 12 million (more than London), the Stadium is in the North-eastward - diagonally opposite from the Hotel - and 20 to 30 kilometres distant. The only possible time for a visit was before 9 a.m. the next morning, and the round trip I was told would take about 2½ hours!

Resigned to the fact of not being able to make a visit, Deng gave me a description of the Stadium and also some other pointers. Apparently the Club formerly played at the Jiangwan Stadium which still exists - and was even further from the Hotel! It is bigger than the current Ground and is located in the Wujiaochang district, near to Fujan University. There are plans to build a new Stadium, with a capacity for 60,000 in the newly developing Pudong area, East of the Huangpu River. Deng is a Manchester United fan also (who isn't these days!) and after our interesting chat I made for my bed. But, I awoke early the next morning, did some time calculations, and at 6.15 a.m. decided 'come or Hell or high water' I would go to the Ground. Having expressed doubts for my sanity (not for the first time), my wife agreed to find out and leave details of where Lunch would be that day. The morning sightseeing didn't promise a lot, therefore should I not return in time I would endeavour get a taxi to our midday rendevouz.

Deng was on duty in the lobby, and after his instructions to a taxi driver I was on my way. Most people would see this as a mad excursion (except possibly you, the reader), however a trip such as this with the early morning traffic (as always very congested) does take you to places and to sights that the 'normal' tourist never sees. My driver whisked me across the City, dodging the worst jams, ducking into side streets, doubling back where necessary, and within 45 minutes we had reached my goal. The first impression of Hong Kou Stadium - near Zhongshan Road (the main bypass) - is of a large and neat Stadium, with two impressive carved elephants guarding the main entrance.

It first looked as if my photo's would have to be taken through spyholes in different gates, but eventually I found opposite the main Stand easy access to the interior. This side consisted of shallow rows of blue seats (individual but without backs), topped by a second tier, with what appeared to be living quarters at the back - again! To my left the seats - now coloured yellow -swept round the end of the Stadium, with a large sporting action monument and a video screen behind this goal. The Main Stand was pitch length, with a part cantilevered roof covering two tiers of seating, including a central portion obviously for dignitaries, and complete with a large Press area at the back. The other end also contained open seating, and I understand the capacity is 38,000. There are four large floodlight pylons, a small training pitch outside, and an impressive enclosed sports hall alongside. The visit was made the more poignant for the plaintive sounds of a trumpet, its owner practising (with the emphasis on practise) in the early morning calm. The return trip to the Hotel was made amidst even more traffic, and after several exciting near-encounters, I arrived back with ten minutes to spare - plenty of time for a hearty breakfast! The 2½ hour round journey by taxi had cost £7-50, including a good tip.

Market day in Suzhou.

I should have had no difficulty in finding the Stadium in Suzhou, our next stop, but I contrived to make a hard job of it. I had no map of this small town (only 300,000 population!), but the sight of one in the Hotel confirmed that the Stadium was only a kilometre or so up the road. Having arrived at the Suzhou Hotel - it was located on the Eastern outskirts of the City, and unusual in that it was located in a large park - in the afternoon, there was an hour or two to explore that day. After a 15 minute walk, enduring a barrage of souvenir sellers (unfortunately a feature of China these days) I had reached, I thought, Wusa Road. The Ground should have been a couple of hundred kilometres off this road, but there was nothing. I then approached a European, on a hired Bicycle (I had considered doing this myself), who turned out to be Danish. A study of her map (she was quite attractive, and there was the temptation to abandon the Ground search!), indicated that Wusa Road was one block further on. However this proved wrong and a trek all around the area still did not produce a Stadium. Having by now reached the main street, South Renmin Road, I had definitely passed the goal somewhere en route.

Another European - this time French - attempted to get some information for me from some locals, who confidently pointed, in the wrong direction I was sure! Disconsolate I made my way back to the Hotel, for it was feeding time - I had failed.

The following morning offered the only chance for another attempt, and with an hour or so to spare, after an early breakfast plus another study of the Hotel map, I set out again. This time I found the Stadium without difficulty, my earlier attempts hadn't taken into account the many roads that existed but were not shown on the map! The effort was well worth it, for this was a Stadium different again from those seen previously. It was market day, and stallholders were setting out their wares down one side, and partly on, the pitch. The Main side of the Stadium consists of a central fully glass-enclosed and roofed area, with high concrete terracing each side, which taper away to nothing at the ends. The terracing was presumably used for either standing or sitting. Each end was flat, with two storey flats behind one goal that gave direct access to the playing area!

Opposite the main Stand there was a peculiar five row bank of terracing which was raised about 1.5 metres above the ground level, making access possible only on the halfway line, where a main entrance to the ground was situated. There were no floodlights, and I would estimate a Ground capacity of around 8,000.

The pitch had seen better days, as had the netless goalposts, and it appeared that football was not an important pastime in Suzhou. A town in the Jiangsu Province, I suppose it is possible that the occasional First Division game could be staged here. At one corner of the Stadium there was an impressive building, the 'Hostel of Physical Culture'.

The unusual Main Stand with its tapering side terraces - like a gigantic truncated pyramid!

- And the view along that side.

Opposite the Main Stand - the 'high level' terrace (beind the market stalls)

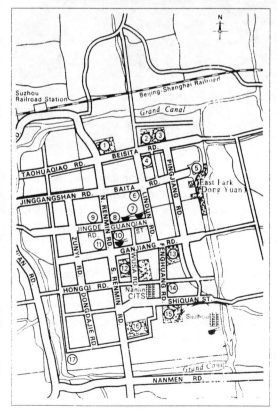

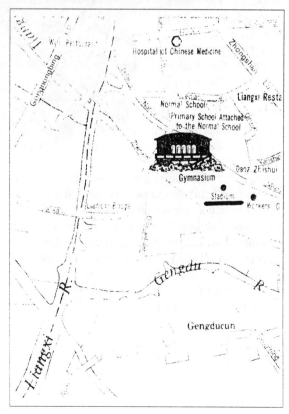

Suzhou Street Plan (The Stadium - '12')　　　**Wuxi Street Plan** - A brief view only of this one

The New and the Old in Wuxi

We were supposed to make the short journey to Wuxi by boat on the Grand Canal, but despite being an enormous waterway (at least 100 metres wide), there had been a water traffic jam on it for four days, which was expected to last for some time! A coach journey instead at least gave us the chance to see some of the countryside between towns, and also see for ourselves the incredible sight of hundreds of barges locked immobile at several points along the route.

No more than two quick photo's from the bus as we passed the construction.

Wuxi, I had already accepted, would be the one City where there was no hope of easily reaching the Stadium. We stayed for one night in the Hubin Hotel, which is attractively located beside the Lihu Lake, but about 6 kilometres from the City centre, where the tourist map showed the location of the Stadium - this was to be a day off. But my luck held, for on our journey to the centre the following day, low and behold we passed close to a new Stadium under construction. I would not have been popular if I had suggested that we stop and do some sightseeing here, and therefore my inspection could only consist of a brief look in passing, and two hurriedly taken photographs from the coach.

This Stadium will be quite impressive when it is finished. It looked similar to a smaller version of the Workers Stadium in Beijing, although probably predominantly open seating, but with a raised cantilevered covered Stand on one side.

I would imagine that the capacity will be in the region of 40,000 and therefore eminently suitable for (Jiangsu) First Division football. It is located South of the City, at the junction of Hubin Lu (Road) and Xisu Lu.

But this was not the end of Stadium's that day, for en route between our sightseeing spots that day, I caught a glimpse of the 'old' Stadium beside the Jiangyuan Creek, off Zhenxin Lu. No chance for any photo's, and just the briefest glance revealed a large covered Stand on one side with open terracing on the other, each about two-thirds pitch length. So Wuxi wasn't so barren for Ground viewing for me as I had anticipated it would be.

Lost in China

Our next stop involved another rail journey, and a short ride to Nanjing; from Shanghai we had travelled 300 km. North-west. Nanjing has featured prominently in Chinese history, having on more than one occasion been the Capital, and perhaps remembered mostly for the terrible slaughter that was undertaken by the Japanese, literally the 'Rape of Nanking', where, in addition over a four day period the aggressors slaughtered 100,000 of the City's occupants. But on to football matters, and this was to be the easiest of all Stadiums to find and explore - how wrong can you be! Having a street plan in advance and being able to locate our Hotel on it - The Central - I discovered the Wutaishan Stadium was no more than a kilometre or so away.

An early rise saw me leaving the Hotel at 6.30 a.m., a full 2½ hours for the journey and plenty of time for breakfast afterwards. Unfortunately, the map had few road names marked on it, and the Stadium was not exactly located. However, in the early morning dim light and drizzle, umbrella in one hand and map in the other I left the Hotel and turned left onto the main Zhongyang Road - or so I thought - not recognising it from the evening before when I had seen it only in the dark. Left at the next main road, and the Stadium should be just a few hundred metres down this large (unnamed thoroughfare). But it wasn't. Surrounded by tall buildings it was impossible to see any likely Stadium structure, but a little more exploring, I thought, would soon enable me locate my goal. A left here, a right there - the few road names meant nothing - and before I knew it I was hopelessly lost! Some school children proved that they don't all learn English in China, for my questions were greeted with bemused, and certain amused, looks. Thinking that I was now walking at least parallel with the road in which our Hotel was situated, I tried a very well dressed young lady, and she actually understood me. She assured me I was a long way from the Stadium and that it would need two bus rides to get there. Nonsense I thought, she obviously couldn't read maps. So I set off on what I thought was the route back to The Central, for by now my time left had been reduced to little over an hour.

Panic began to set in - a completely alien City, no landmarks, no traceable road names, no idea where the hell I was. Eventually I came across two motorized rickshaws, and one of the drivers - after a scan of my map - assured me (the 'conversation' carried out in sign language) that he could take me there - at a cost of 2 yuan (about 12p). We set off amongst the ever noisy traffic, in what I was sure was the opposite direction, before we finally stopped at a Hotel - but not the Central! But at least they would speak English there, so I climbed out of the whicker seat, and discovered that he now wanted 20 yuan for the 5 minute ride (probably equivalent to a day's wages). Our argument began to encourage a crowd, so I settled for 10 yuan, even if he didn't, and proceeded to the Hotel lobby. Better than English speaking Chinese, some Americans informed me that I was just a block or two away from The Central. But I had done enough walking already, and with my confidence severely shaken, I took a taxi. I have never seen such a welcoming sight as this, when we drove up to The Central Hotel. At this point I discovered that there were two similar exits from the Hotel, at right angles to each other - and two hours earlier, I of course had chosen the wrong one! My nightmare trip did teach me one important lesson though, always take a sheet of (Chinese) headed notepaper, or card, with you - words such as 'Central Hotel', will mean nothing to the locals, but the unreadable (to us) Chinese writing will be recognised.

I never did see this Stadium, which I anticipated would be a large one. But my record of one Stadium per Chinese stopping-place was not broken, for on our departure by air to Beijing later that day, I saw a consolation one from above.

Nanjing - there should have been no difficulty in finding the Wutaishan Stadium!

Taking a Peak in Beijing.

The Doyen of Chinese Grounds - The Workers Stadium, Beijing.

The Workers Stadium, Beijing, was the football shrine that I had looked forward to, but imagine my disappointment when I discovered that it was located about 20 km. from our Hotel on the other side of this vast Capital.

No entry via Gongrentiyuchang Beilu

But also imagine my joy, and unbelievable luck, when we stopped for an early dinner en route to the Hotel (at 5.30 p.m.!), when we parked off Gongren Tiyuchang and within site of the Stadium. I had only 30 minutes or so for this one, and a short brisk walk took me to the main entrance, where the large forecourt was used by the local kite-flying fraternity. These were the first kites I had seen in China (the hobby appears to be confined mainly to Beijing), but I didn't have time to hire one for a flight - which the locals were doing rather than arriving with their own models. But to my dismay no amount of persuading could convince the guard on duty that he should let me through the gate to the Stadium. Another brisk walk took me to an alternative entrance (off Xindong Lu), where there was no closed gate and no guard, just chess and card players along the entrance path. But fate decreed that I was not to get inside.

The Stadium is an enormous ellipse of concrete , with the end of the terrace extending over the top of the high columned wall. Within the wall there are about 30 exits, and an amazing collection of non-football related businesses - a Hotel, a Hairdressers, and other various shops. I walked about a third way round the perimeter before finding a clear opening between the columns that led directly to the interior.

Inside the perimeter - the high columned wall

But once again no amount of imploring would convince the guards that I just **had** to see inside. However there was a consolation prize, for a short way further round I was able to glimpse the inside through a badly fitting pair of gates. It really is impressive, with 80,000 backless individual seats in two tiers. Only part of the upper tier is covered - a continuous cantilever concrete ring - except for two pitch-length runs opposite each other where the roof also extends to cover the complete upper tier. The floodlights run along these two extended roof edges. I returned to the Restaurant in time for a only a quick drink, but in all honesty at that time I really wasn't hungry - two bananas bought on my return from the Stadium sufficed - and as my luck would have it most of our party had the 'Peking Runs' the next day - but not I!

And so to the last Stadium on my whistle-stop tour. The 'Grand View Hotel' is in the South-east area of Beijing, and by another stroke of good fortune, it was no more than 5 km. from the Xiankongtan Stadium, an impressive venue, and probably the number two Ground in Beijing. After passing close by that evening, and twice more the next day whilst doing our sightseeing, I determined that this was one I also had to see at close range. So to the last day, plenty of time after an early breakfast, but how to get there?

I've always considered that resorting to a taxi ride is cheating. Walk or take a bus if possible, but on the this occasion I succumbed - and 'cheated'. For just 8 yuan including a tip (about 50p), I made it. But once again to my disappointment, the guards on duty just wouldn't let me in - a problem I had not encountered elsewhere in China. But at least I saw at close range this somewhat ornate sporting venue. A modern, and inevitable oval shaped concrete structure, not unlike the Workers Stadium but on a smaller scale. At the main entrance, off Yongdingmen Xi, there is a goalpost shaped red arch, and a rectangular building sprouting out of the top of the Stadium wall at this point. The terraced seating appeared to be uncovered except on one side which had a pitch length roof, and outside the walls stand four traditional large floodlight pylons. Although I never got inside, it was none the less a good Stadium at which to end my groundhopping.

I did have the name of an English speaking Official at the Chinese F.A. (which is located at 9 Tiyuguan Road - the Mandarin word translates as 'Stadium' I was told) - but much as I would liked to have paid a visit, I wasn't going to miss the Great Wall, The Forbidden City, etc. - where, at these places, there appeared to be no Football Grounds.

The colourful entrance to the Xian Nong Tan Stadium

Geographical location of the Clubs

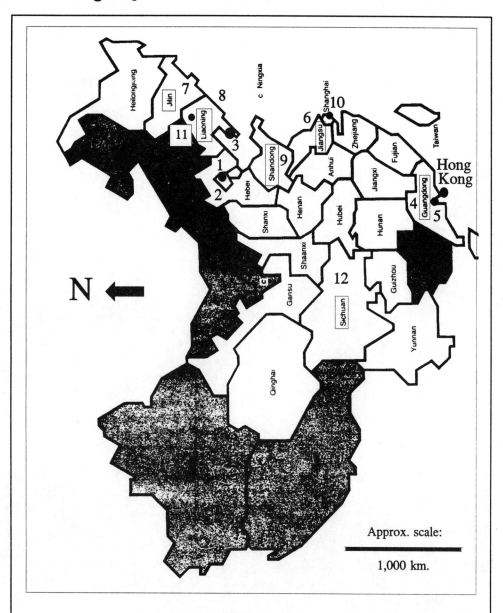

1st Division:

1. Ba Yi (1st August)
2. Beijing
3. Dalian
4. Guangdong *
5. Guangzhou
6. Jiangsu
7. Jilin *
8. Liaoning *
9. Shangdong *
10. Shanghai
11. Shenyang
12. Sichuan *

(* indicates a Province team)

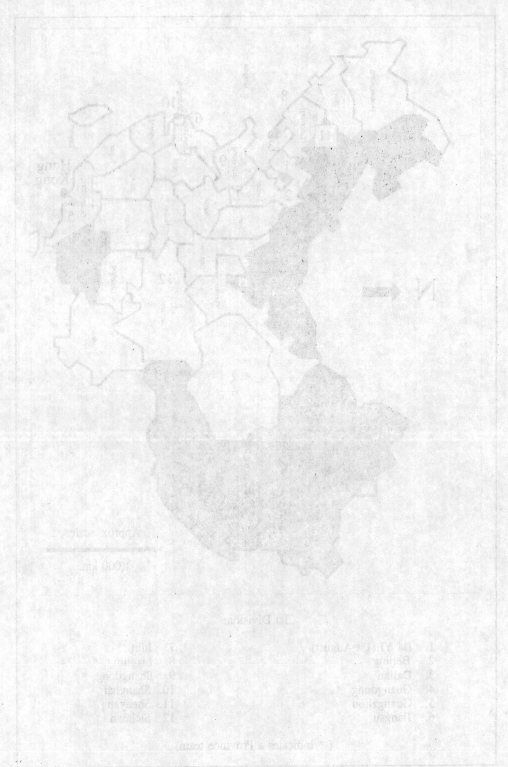